THE BROTHERHOOD OF THE BADGE

My Time Walking The Blue Line

C. R. Holbert

DEDICATION

This book is dedicated to those
Brothers and Sisters across the country
who every day strap a gun around their
waist
and pin a badge on their chest
in an attempt to make this a better and
safer world in which we live.

Stay Safe.

TABLE OF CONTENTS

*The last chapter is an excerpt from the first
book in my new fiction Series,
"The Trooper".*

*Nate Johnson is a retired State Trooper
fighting bad guys and the demons that
come with over twenty years of wading
through the violence, blood, and guts of the
backwoods of West Virginia. After losing his
best friend to an ambush, and now working
as a private investigator, Nate takes on the
rough cases no one else will touch. Working
with vengeful like determination, Nate is
often left wondering,
"Which side of the law am I walking now?"*

Preface

This is not another book filled with police stories about violent crimes. Yes, there are some of those in here, but I wanted this publication to be different. I wanted to give the reader different insight to the violence and stress endured by many of our law enforcement officers every day from my perspective and my own personal experiences and feelings.

The names used in this publication are fictitious and meant to protect certain parties. In some instances small details have been left out or slightly altered, again in an attempt to protect the identities and lives of the individuals involved.

We always see the stories where the bad guy is in prison and the officer is a hero. But what happens in the after math? What happens when the officer goes home at the end of his or her shift and tries to explain why a small child had to blow out their birthday candles with one parent not there. People don't realize the stress does not end with the officer and it does not stop at the end of the shift. The stress of being an officer involves the entire family and sometimes everyone has to suffer.

The mental and emotional side of law enforcement is not often talked about. It's not a topic we are supposed to bring up. We are supposed to keep those things in check. It's only been in the recent years departments have started setting up counseling for their officers. Only recently have officers started getting the outlets they deserve and need.

There is a lot of talk and programs for Veterans suffering from PTSD and rightfully so. However we are way behind in offering the help needed to law enforcement, fire, and EMS personnel. The 911 tragedies have brought some of the need to light in recent years, but more is needed as the world becomes an increasingly violent place.

I hope in writing this, people will gain a little better understanding into the stresses involved in the every day life of a Trooper, Deputy, and City Police Officer. And just as importantly, the pressure put on the families, and the lasting effects of day after day in dealing with life altering tragedies in one form or another.

I would challenge you to consider something; most people only suffer true life altering events once or twice in their lives. Law Enforcement Officers deal with those same tragedies almost daily as they try to make this a little better world for everybody to live. It's impossible to deal with the death, violence, and emotions of these events and not be effected ourselves. It's impossible to see and experience the things we do and not take the emotions and stress home with us.

I hope to bring some of these things to light as you read this, to give you a small glimpse into the emotions and mindset involved in walking the blue line.

John 15:13

In the middle of the compound at the West Virginia State Police Academy rests a small, nondescript monument marker. The monument is white and bears simple lettering, "John 15:13, Greater Love Hath No Man Than This, That A Man Lay Down His Life For His Friends."

Those simple words embody the camaraderie felt between law enforcement officers from coast to coast in this Country. There is camaraderie that people do not and can not fully understand unless they have been a part of it. A camaraderie that runs deep and strong within the men and women who protect and serve this great country every day.

It says a lot to know the person beside you will jump in front of a bullet for you and you in turn would do the same for them. It's a huge sense of pride and an awesome feeling of responsibility.

Think about the people you work with every day. How many of them would you willingly give your life for? Even better, how many do you feel would give their life for you? How many would you embrace and be proud to call Brother or Sister?

In the Brotherhood of Law Enforcement, you don't have to think about it, you just know it's there. You know the person beside you will fight to the death with you and for you. He or she in turn has the same feeling of Brotherhood for you.

In West Virginia, all law enforcement officers go through the State Police Academy located in Institute. The county deputies, city officers, and Department of Natural Resources Officers go through a sixteen week course. All State Troopers attend a separate twenty six week cadet program.

There are several distinct advantages in training all officers within one institution together in the same classes. You are guaranteed to have all officers within the state trained in the same techniques and in an identical manner. You also have solid control over how that training is administered, monitored, and updated.

The advantages extend well after the students graduate from their programs. Since students attend the Academy with officers from around the state, good working relationships are fostered between multiple departments. As an officer, it is very often you may have to work a case that crosses into different areas of the State. There is a good chance you already know somebody in that jurisdiction. The fact you both have been trained in the same evidence collection and interrogation techniques will only enhance your investigation.

The Academy programs are conducted in a strict paramilitary manner. Students arrive on Sunday afternoons and stay through Friday evening. There are no telephones, televisions, or radios allowed. A typical day starts at five in the morning and it is common to have students in classes until ten at night. Of course there are those certain nights when the students also have night watches. Sleep can get to be a much cherished commodity.

It is a heavily stressed induced atmosphere that forces the students to learn how to function as a team. Students learn very quickly to rely on each other for support. If one fails, the entire class fails and suffers the misery. The team also succeeds as one unit and all students share the rewards.

This environment cultivates deep feelings of camaraderie and unity that lasts long past the graduation ceremonies. This is the reason when an officer in one department falls, the loss is always felt through out the entire state.

In West Virginia, the feeling of Brotherhood is not reserved for just your own department. It includes every department, Trooper, Deputy, and Officer within the confines of the State.

In comparison as a US Navy Deep Sea Diver, I completed some of the toughest and most demanding schools the military has to offer. When I earned my Dive Pin, it was truly a monumental day in my life.

After ten weeks of Boot Camp in Orlando, Florida, I was sent to Great Lakes, Illinois for Hospital Corps School. Afterwards, I then spent six months at Coronado, California for Second Class Deep Sea School. Once I had earned my Second Class Dive pin, I worked at the small base clinic in Panama City, Florida for almost four months awaiting the next step in my continued training.

I then completed my training in Advanced Diving Medicine before graduating from First Class Deep Sea School at the Naval Diving and Salvage Training Center. It was approximately one and a half years of training before I earned my Deep Sea Diving Medical Technician Dive Pin.

Years later after my discharge from the NAvy, I was talking to a friend I had been stationed with in Virginia Beach while still on active duty. He started asking me about my experiences at the State Police Academy as compared to Dive School. My Buddy had a hard time believing me when I tried to explain how much tougher my experience had been during my law enforcement training. While it had not been as physically demanding as Dive School, the mental and academic stress, made the Police Academy over all more difficult.

I am a graduate of both the basic and cadet programs. I spent a total of forty two weeks in both programs. Not only were these weeks filled with induced stress, they were also spent away from my family.

In West Virginia, you may have already graduated from the sixteen weeks Basic Class. However, you still have to complete the entire Cadet program to be a State Trooper. Hence the forty two weeks spent in training at the Academy.

When I was an instructor at the Academy, we would spend the first several weeks breaking the students down as we would prepare to build them back up into West Virginia Officers, Deputies, and Troopers.

By the end of the second week, the students were tired and stressed. In preparation for the build up phase and really bringing the class together as one team, I would take the class to the monument on Thursday night, right before they went to bed.

I circled them around the white marker and would read its inscription very slowly and deliberately. Then we would discuss what it meant to place your life in another's hands and the responsibility when that same person put their life in your hands. After that night, you could often see a difference in the way the class would come together as a team.

By the end of their program, whether a basic or cadet class, the students are literally ready to stand shoulder to shoulder and fight the evil of the world to the end. These men and women have trained hard for months and learned the intimate strengths and weaknesses of each other. They have also learned a lot about their own constitution and determination.

In the last week of each program, the classes are given a prime rib dinner the night before graduation. It is quite a feast and at one point, the students are given the opportunity to have some fun at the instructor's expense by doing impressions of the staff. I have seen some pretty funny impressions and skits at my own expense.

As the evening festivities came to a close, and the students prepared to hit their racks, I would call the class to the monument. I always wanted to end the class at what I felt was the place it really got started. As we would gather around the simple white marker, I reminded them of where we had started and where we were now, as a class, as a team, and as Brothers and Sisters.

It would always end with me shaking each student's hand and addressing them as Brother or Sister.

I always felt very close to every student that graduated in one of my classes. I still take great pride when I see a news article or story involving somebody I had a hand in training or mentoring.

I always get great satisfaction in seeing the development from being rookies into mentors and leaders themselves, within their own departments.

One of the classes I taught at the Academy was Water Survival. It was basically a week in the swimming pool learning life saving and survival techniques. I was often surprised at the number of adult men and women who could not swim. However, by the end of the week, each student could enter the pool in full uniform, tread water for a period of time, and then swim a full length of the pool.

This would be a huge accomplishment for several individuals, as some had not even been able to swim several days before. At the West Virginia State Police Academy, if you can't pass the swim test, then you don't graduate the Cadet program.

I had one student that was absolutely terrified of the water. I thought he was going to pass out just from having to jump into the shallow end of the pool. However, his desire to be a West Virginia State Trooper outweighed his phobia of the water. With a lot of one on one instruction, he slowly came around. By the time of his swim test, we surprised the rest of the class as he actually did a flip from the diving platform into the pool. The whole class cheered and slapped him on the back. I don't know who was more proud of his accomplishment, me or him?

I remember not long after one particular class graduated, seeing a news story in which a former student had jumped into a river and saved a woman from drowning. As a class supervisor and swimming instructor you can't help but feel great pride. The pride that a little piece of knowledge you imparted on a student ended up saving the life of another.

Once, I had a former student call and relay to me how they had saved a woman who was choking on her pizza one evening at a restaurant. Again, I felt a huge sense of pride because he had been successful using a skill I taught in my First Aid/First Responder Class.

The Bond of the Brotherhood is one than can not be seen, but it is very real nonetheless. The Bond is a feeling of family, family you are willingly devoted to and would readily give your life for. The feelings of mutual loyalty run deeper than the Grand Canyon.

The Police Academy is the all too important part of planting those seeds of devotion between Brothers and Sisters in Blue. When you have completed the program and walked across the stage to get your certificate, you have earned something no one can ever take away from you, the right to walk the line.

Twisted Metal

Being a certified accident reconstructionist, I was often called to some of the most horrific wrecks imaginable. It was my job to put the pieces together and be able to tell exactly what occurred. Which vehicle or pedestrian was where, at what time, traveling which direction, and at what speeds. There were a slew of other fine details also, often writing a time line report broken down by the tenths of seconds.

By the tenth of a second? Yes, by the tenth of a second. You would be surprised by the velocity of a vehicle how much it will travel in one tenth of a second, much less a full second.

Here's how it works, think of a vehicle traveling fifty five miles per hour, it will realistically travel fifty five miles in one hour's time. That is the speed of the vehicle. If you convert that speed mathematically to velocity, the same vehicle is traveling at eighty feet per second. A lot can happen in that eighty feet, a lot of carnage and death. Even if you break it down to tenths of a second, that car will still move eight feet in that amount of time.

Countless studies have concluded on a normal day, under average conditions, the reaction time of the human driver to be 1.6 seconds. That is 1.6 seconds from the time the driver sees the anomaly, the brain to process the information, and then for the body to react. And what is the vehicle doing in that time? Still traveling of course.

Simple math concludes the car will travel one hundred twenty feet before the driver can even get their foot on the brake. Then you have to factor in the braking time of the vehicle before it can even get stopped. That's a lot of distance for things to get torn up and destroyed, whether it's metal or flesh. Think about that the next time you're on the interstate traveling over seventy miles an hour. Do you really have enough distance from the car in front of you?

In the human body there are two main arteries that run to a person's lower extremities, carrying oxygen rich blood from the lungs. If one of these arteries gets cut a person could bleed out in less than a minute as the pressure from the beating heart pushes the bright red blood out of the body. If both of these pipelines of life get cut at the same time, then a person will bleed out and die literally in a matter of seconds.

If a person has an extremely heavy weight fall on them, sometimes one or both of those arteries will get cut. However, death does not immediately follow. What happens is the heavy weight not only cuts the artery, but pinches it closed like a tourniquet. As long as the weight stays on the artery, the life giving blood stays in the body. But, when the weight is removed, the arteries open wide and the person will die in seconds.

There is no way to prevent it.

In the state of West Virginia, tractor trailer combinations can be granted a higher weight limit on certain roadways. Normally a tractor trailer is maxed at eighty thousand pounds, on some roads, while hauling coal, that limit is pushed to over one hundred twenty five thousand pounds. That's almost a fifty thousand pound increase, and the extra weight can absolutely increase the carnage exponentially.

I was dispatched to a coal truck roll over, the first thing one winter morning. It had snowed several inches the previous evening and now the temperature was just above freezing. The snow was still on the ground, but it was turning pretty slushy.

The roll over was way up into the head of a hollow on a small two lane road. The fully loaded truck had been coming down a steep grade when the brakes failed. The driver attempted to steer onto a runaway truck ramp in an effort to stop his increasing rate of speed. What he didn't see under the fresh snow was a drain culvert sitting directly in his path. The culvert had an iron grate over it, but was about three feet lower than the adjacent roadway. When the front tires hit the culvert, the steering assembly on the big truck disintegrated. The truck shot to the left and straight up at about a seventy degree angle on a steep slope beside the road.

The truck rolled to the right causing the driver to fall out through the passenger side window. The man landed on his back atop of the cold, slushy, muddy blacktop. Then the extremely heavy truck fell on top of the poor driver, crushing him from his stomach down.

It took me approximately twenty minutes of hard driving to get to the scene. The ambulance and I arrived at the same time, the medics and I got out of our vehicles and hurried to the wreck. When I surveyed the damage, we found the driver on his back lying on the roadway with the truck on its right side. The poor man was pinned by the tractor's frame directly behind the cab and in front of the trailer. He was still alive and talking to those around him.

The fire department was working at a furious rate trying to crib the truck and get the lift bags under the frame.

We quickly cleared the area of unnecessary people and went to work on the injured man. It took about two seconds before the medic and I looked at each other and shook our heads. We both knew what was going to happen as soon as the firemen got the air bags under the frame and started to lift the truck. When the weight was lifted, the crushed arteries were going to open up and this guy was going to bleed out internally in a matter of seconds.

We both took a step back and discussed a plan of action. We were going to give this guy the best chance to survive as possible.

We called for a helicopter transport as we were approximately twenty minutes out from the nearest trauma center.

Then, the word came, the helicopter would not transport, since the victim was going to be a traumatic arrest patient. He was going to have to be transported on the ground.

So we backed the ambulance as close as we could to the rolled over truck and cleared a path out of the area. We even had a volunteer fireman waiting in the driver's seat so both medics could be free to work on the patient. The MAST trousers were laid out so we could get the driver in them as fast as possible to try to stop as much bleeding as possible. IV's were started and oxygen was flowing as we tried to prep the victim for the move. All of this was done in a matter of minutes as the fire department never slowed down their efforts to lift the truck.

I laid in the slush with the driver and tried to keep him calm as the activity around him was moving at a fast rate. He told me he was in his sixties and had been driving big trucks all his life. He had several million miles of safe driving under his belt and this was his first accident.

When I was trained in combat medicine in the Navy, one thing we were always taught, you never take away a person's will to live. You never look at an injured person and say, "You are not going to make it." The human body and spirit can survive things that defy all medical logic.

So, even though I knew the percentage of survival for the driver was extremely slim, I was not going to tell him that. I was not going to be the one to take away his desire to live.

As we talked, he asked me several times to please get the truck off his legs. I told him the fire department was working as hard as they could. Even though he looked forward to getting the truck lifted, I was dreading what I knew was going to happen.

I heard the compressor start up as I knew the air bags were now under the frame. The medic looked at me and nodded his head. It was time. I told the man the truck was about to lift off, he thanked me.

As soon as the truck frame lifted an inch, his eyes closed.

We moved as fast as we could, the medics were top notch and could not have been asked to do better as we got him on the gurney and ran the short distance to the truck. He flat lined about half way there.

The work never stopped as those two paramedics did everything humanly possible all the way to the hospital trying to save his life. He was pronounced DOA at the hospital.

As for me, the work was really just starting. Even though I felt emotionally exhausted, I still had to complete my accident investigation. It took me an additional two hours to get the entire investigation completed and everything wrapped up.

As soon as I got into my cruiser to leave the scene, I was informed there were messages for me to call the deceased man's family as soon as possible. I told the dispatcher I would take care of it when I returned to the office.

I looked at the clock on my dashboard, it was a little before ten in the morning. I felt like it should be later in the afternoon. God, it was going to be a long day.

When I finally got back to the office, I tried to call the family back and was connected with voice mail. I left a message and went to work finishing my fatality report.

It wasn't long before I was called to the front waiting area by the secretary, as the deceased man's son and daughter were there to see me. I gave the siblings my condolences after shaking hands and escorted them back to my office.

We talked briefly as I gave them what information I could at the time. Then the son asked. "Was my dad still alive when you got there?"

"Yes, he was alive and talking."

"What message did he give you to tell us?"

"Excuse me?"

"What were his final words to us?"

I tried to explain to them there were no final death bed messages their father asked me to deliver.

"I'm sure you knew he was probably going to die, right?"

"We were busy trying to do everything we could to save your father's life."

"Surely you told him he was about to die. I know Dad would have left last words for us once he knew he was going to die. What were they?"

I tried to explain the concept of giving a person every fighting tool to survive and never taking away the spirit and desire to fight to live.

They were having a very hard time believing there was no death bed devotion of family love from their father. I know they wanted to hear some final outcry of love for his children, but it just didn't happen. I hate to say it, but his last words were not of his children, he just asked for us to please get the truck off him.

One day I drove up on a box truck that had rolled over in the median. It had just occurred and the dust was still settling as I came to a stop and turned my blue lights on. The truck was lying on its driver's side across the grassy median. We had been having a lot of rain the past several days and I could see the trenches left in the mud as the truck's tires lost traction causing the roll over.

I ran toward the cab of the truck to check on the driver and see if there were any passengers. I was surprised when I looked through the cracked windshield to see the cab was empty of anybody. I felt a pit in my stomach as I ran around the truck looking for the ejected driver. Not finding anybody lying around the truck, I got on my knees and started looking underneath. Then I saw his feet underneath the area between the cargo box and the cab. I ran back around to what was the roof of the cab and tried to get underneath the truck to check on the ejected driver. The cargo box was one with a big refrigeration unit on the front. The driver was caught in the depression of the median with the refrigeration unit resting on the side of his head. I thought for sure he was certainly dead, and then I heard him moan. He was alive and calling for help!

I ran and got an old US Army issue folding shovel from the trunk of my cruiser and ran back to the scene. About that time, another Trooper pulled up and we made ourselves busy trying to get underneath the truck to the driver. It actually took very little effort to get the man from under the heavy truck. Luckily the ground had been very soft and the refrigeration unit had only applied enough his pressure to his head to keep him trapped. Once we moved his head slightly, we were able to slide him right out.

I was amazed this man had been ejected from the cab of his truck, the truck had fallen on his head, and other than a red spot on his temple, was pretty much uninjured. He was just as surprised as we were. He said he only remembered the truck rolling, him falling out the window, and then the truck landing on his head.

While I did witness several amazing survivals from horrendous accidents, some of the goriest things I witnessed resulted from vehicle collisions. There were collisions with other vehicles, trees, guardrails, and even farm animals.

I once saw a pickup truck with a load of pigs get turned over on the road and then several of the pigs were struck by another vehicle. Just when you think you have seen about everything, you roll up and there are firemen running around an accident scene chasing pigs. What did I do, you ask? Got out and helped chase the pigs, what else? I never knew pigs could be so hard to catch. By the time we got them all rounded up, I looked like I had been in a fight with a grizzly bear.

The one thing I did enjoy about an accident scene was the challenge of putting the pieces of the puzzle back together again. Figuring out exactly what happened by examining the tire marks and vehicle damage.

Accident reconstruction, to me, is a fascinating field of study. It involves a lot of advanced math and physics into being able to determine vehicle speeds and damage analysis.

Being on the Accident Reconstruction Team, is why I was called to so many accident scenes, both by my department and others as well. It was common for me to be at several fatality crashes in different parts of the state on top of my regular duties each week. Even when I was stationed at the Academy, I still went out and worked quite a few accident scenes.

Even though I liked the challenge of figuring out what had happened in a wreck, there was still the human factor involved. The lifeless bodies ejected, the bodies trapped within the twisted metal, and the survivors.

There was nothing worse than trying to perform first aid on victims and having a family member arrive at the scene. You're trying to triage who you can help and who you cannot and a hysterical loved one comes running up adding stress to an already chaotic scene. Sometimes it was very difficult keeping order if there was no help.

Usually when it comes to accident scenes, everything is happening very fast. You are trying to get the victims in the ambulances as quick as possible, and everything wrapped up so the road can be opened back up. It's not until afterwards when you have a moment to sit in your cruiser and take a breath, do you really have an opportunity to comprehend what you just witnessed.

And of course there is no time to process the carnage you just experienced, because there are usually already several other calls waiting for you as soon as you get freed up.

I had one citizen call and complain to my Sergeant because he did not feel I had expressed enough concern over the fact his neighbor kept putting their garbage bags in his refuse cans. The neighbor wasn't dumping the garbage on his property, he was just putting his garbage in the other's cans.

To be honest, I couldn't care less about the neighbor putting garbage in cans that did not belong to him. I know that sounds bad, but the man was adamant I arrest his neighbor. There was nothing I could arrest him for at all. I talked to the neighbor who agreed not to do it anymore. However, it was not enough for the original complainant. He just could not understand why the law would not allow me to arrest the neighbor. I finally had to leave which only enhanced the guy's anger.

What he did not know is I had just left a bad accident scene in which one person had died and several others were barely hanging on to thin strands of their lives. I had just lifted the lifeless form of a lady from a van as her husband was screaming for her to not die. It was excruciatingly painful as we tried to get the man in the ambulance against his wishes as he wanted to know the condition of his wife. As we are not doctors, we can not determine when a person is officially dead. We were still trying everything possible to revive her, so he was sent to the hospital without knowing the condition of his wife.

In the meantime, Mr. Pissed-Off Citizen had been waiting almost an hour for me to arrive since he had called 911, because somebody was putting trash in his cans. He had actually called 911 two more times before I was able to get there. So of course, he was as mad as a wet hen when I arrived.

It only made him angrier, I was on my cell phone sitting in his driveway before I got out of my cruiser. It did not help his case that he kept knocking on my window as I was trying to carry on my conversation.

What he did not know, was I was actually talking to the county 911 dispatcher, who was telling me the lady had officially been declared dead. I had been on my way to talk to the victim's family at the hospital and stopped at his house on my way due to his repeated calls and impatience over some garbage cans. To be honest, I don't think he would have cared if I would have tried to explain it to him.

As soon as I stepped out of my cruiser and put my campaign hat on, I was subjected to a berating that most people would not have stood for. He was so mad, I could see the veins standing out on his temples. I stood and gritted my teeth as I listened to this knucklehead remind me that his taxes paid my salary. I briefly thought about asking for a pay raise just to see if I could get one of those throbbing veins to burst.

I briefly looked down as this guy furiously continued his rant and noticed there was mud on my freshly polished boots and uniform pants leg. Mud I had gotten from kneeling in the ditch beside the road trying to help get a dead lady out of a twisted up van. I looked up and stared at this idiot and exercised every bit of control to keep from punching him right in the mouth.

There must have been a little something to my look as he finally quit talking. Of course part of his complaint was I acted angry because he had wanted to make a report. At that point, I couldn't help but think about my impending trip to the hospital to talk to the victim's family.

It took me about fifteen minutes to talk to the neighbor and try my best to explain to the upset man why I was not taking the neighbor away in the back of my cruiser. The more I tried to explain the law to him, the more he yelled I was not doing my job. He demanded my supervisor's name and my .badge number, which I readily gave. Of course he was on the phone with my Detachment Commander before I was even able to get backed out of his driveway.

When I later returned to the Detachment, I immediately had to type an official response to the angry citizen's complaint to my Troop Captain. Evidently my Detachment Commander's response had not been good enough and the calls had progressed to the

State Police Headquarters in South Charleston.

Before I could even begin work on my fatality accident report, I had to spend an hour typing a two page narrative of exactly everything that had transpired during my time at Mr. Citizen's house. I was required to go into extreme detail to the exact reasons I did not effect an arrest and what steps I had done in an effort to make the upset man satisfied.

I did not receive any kind of official reprimand, however later I did get a talk from my Sergeant about maintaining professional composure at all costs. At least the Detachment Commander was understanding and did his discussion in an effort to mentor my growth as a young Trooper.

Thinking back, I still can't help but wish one of those veins had ruptured.

The Lost Innocence of a Child

A child is the most precious resource we have.

And nobody would ever intentionally hurt a child....right?

I wish I could say that was true.

Some of the biggest atrocities I ever witnessed as a law enforcement officer, involved children. Children beaten, burned, neglected, sexually assaulted you name it, I've probably seen it.

Each of the hundreds of cases I have been involved with had an effect on me. There's no way a person can investigate these types of crimes and not think of their own children at home. There is no greater anguish than to look into the eyes of a six year old child as they describe being forced to have intercourse with an older relative. Or listen to a fourteen year old describe how they were used as currency for sexual favors in a poker game by their step father.

Then there were the victim interviews in which the abused had turned into offenders themselves. Very often committing the same crimes they had been victims of at one time. To compound the tragedy, these abused turned abusers, very often committed their crimes with a lot more anger, hence more violently. Often targeting weaker and smaller children, lashing out with physical violence in retaliation for the pain they had suffered during their own ordeal.

I worked a case once where I interviewed a seventeen year old boy that was a very real eye opener for me. The boy had been in intensive therapy for over a year and was just getting to the point where he could discuss what he had suffered. This kid reminded me of interviewing a long term prison convict, he was very detached and matter of fact. He spoke without emotion as he talked of putting a knife to his younger brother's throat and sodomizing him repeatedly over a period of a year. He told me over and over he loved his brother very much, but it was the only way he knew to get rid of his anger.

Now of course, the younger brother had beaten up a younger family member and committed his own act of sodomy. The younger brother had also started self mutilating him self by slicing his arms with razor blades. The younger boy had stated it was his way of punishing himself for hurting the other family member.

The problem with a case like this is the victim is also an offender. How do you decide a just and fair punishment, they all have suffered terrible lasting mental effects. Sometimes therapy works, but the majority of the time it does not, and the offender will often go on to offend again.

Every victim interview was different and had a lasting impression on me. Sometimes the child would tell what happened in a very matter of fact way, sometimes the child could barely discuss it without crying hysterically. There were times I could barely choke back the tears as I heard stories of unimaginable violations of innocence.

A lot of times the interview of the suspect is even harder to deal with than the victims. In my interviews and interrogations I learned very quickly, most sexual offenders will confess everything if they think the officer understands why they committed the atrocity they did. Imagine sitting face to face with some one as they describe in intimate detail of having sexual intercourse with a ten year old. "Sure, I understand exactly why you would want to have sex with a ten year old. Tell me all about it, after all, in today's time, ten year girls look a lot older than they actually are. I don't blame you for doing it at all, now tell me all about it in your confession. Sign here please."

I know, right now you are thinking you wouldn't be nice to the offender, "I'd kick his butt! No way would I be nice to him! He doesn't deserve anything other than castration!"

I agree with your anger and agree in exactly what the offender deserves. However, as soon as you touch that person, you lose the case. Or as soon as he thinks you are mocking him or don't understand his emotions or tendencies, he will clam up and shout for a lawyer. So now, imagine the emotional restraint you have to maintain to keep from cleaning this person's clock as they describe making a young child into a "woman." Or maintain restraint while hearing how the child asked for and deserved what they got.

I worked an abuse case where a thirteen year old boy had gotten caught masturbating by his parents. As punishment, the parents duck taped the boy to a kitchen chair, naked, and made him watch porno movies for several hours as they belt whipped him in the groin area. The parents were astonished I would consider it abuse and both stated it was their prerogative how they punished their child, not mine.

You also have to remember there are just as many cases where the offender is a female and there are just as many cases where the victim is a male. There is no stereotypical sexual offender. I took an FBI course on sexual assaults once, that said the average sexual predator while offend an average of over forty people in their life time. Forty is a huge number compared to how many actually get reported.

I always pursued these cases as far and as hard as I could. It wasn't long before I obtained the reputation as being the "Go to Person" for crimes against children. The Social Workers often came into the Detachment and asked for me by name when they had a child abuse case because they knew it would be worked quickly and efficiently. I was proud of the fact that I had the reputation for being good at working them, however after a while, they began to truly have an effect on me.

I felt like I had to be the protector of these children and be strong for them. I felt guilty about their loss of innocence, an innocence that could never be regained. I wanted so badly to be able to take them from the traumatizing environment they were in and put them somewhere they could enjoy being children. To be able to run and play and not have to worry about being burned with a lighter or smelling the harmful fumes of the family meth lab cooking in the same room they were eating their cheerios.

Child sexual assault cases are among some of the hardest to work, usually due to the lack of evidence. A large majority of cases really come down to the word of a child versus the word of an adult. Sometimes the child is so young, the officer has to let the evidence speak on their behalf.

A lot of child cases don't even involve sex. A child can be just as traumatized from the physical or mental torture they have often been subjected to. I have seen starvation and filthy environment damage many a child, both physically and mentally.

You might think these types of abused children would stay home and never go to school, but you are very wrong. Most of the time school is the only place the child can feel secure and get a good meal to eat. Plus the worthless parents like having the time with the children out of the house so they can divulge in whatever activity they want.

I worked a year as a School Resource Officer when I was a Deputy Sheriff. It was an assignment that truly opened my eyes to the challenges facing our school systems. Ever since then, I have said if you really want to know what is going on with a child, go ask their teacher. Often times the teachers will notice an issue long before the parents. In today's time, the teacher usually spends more time with the child than one or both parents.

I got called to a local elementary school one day because a teacher had found a bag of marijuana in a six year olds' book bag. Six years old! When I talked to the child, he really had no idea what it was other than his daddy smoked it a lot. He just brought it to school to show his friends.

I called the boy's home and talked to his mother. When she learned where the bag of dope was, she went nuts. She demanded I send it home with the child because if not his father was going to mad. She said she was afraid of the whipping the boy was going to get for letting his dad's weed get confiscated.

The boy did not get the drugs back and I made sure I was at the house when dad came home from work. Needless to say, the boy did not get a whipping, and dad took a little trip with me to jail.

One thing I always did in a child case was create a time line of the child's grades and discuss their behavior with the teachers. Humans are creatures of habit and children are no different.

Maybe a child is usually very active and talkative during class and then they become quiet and reserved. Or even the opposite, they are a quiet natured child and then start acting out in unusual ways. Their grades are always a good indication of a change in a child's lifestyle. A straight "A" student who suddenly stops turning in homework is a strong indication of something going on somewhere.

As I would do my timelines and compare when the alleged abused started to the altered activity at school, the times were almost always approximately the same. I would say probably a third of the cases I worked were initiated by a school employee.

One morning as I was on my way to the Quincy State Police Detachment, I got a call of an out of control twelve year old. The parents were requesting Law Enforcement because they could not control their son and he was refusing to go to school. Great, I thought, what a way to start the day.

As I pulled up to the residence, I couldn't help but notice the disarray of the yard and the trash strewn about. I walked to the door and was greeted by the boy's parents. As I entered the house, the smell was overpowering and there were cockroaches running everywhere. There was rotted food sitting on the counter and the sink was buried under piles of dirty dishes and trash. Needless to say, the smell inside was not very pleasant.

The parents proceeded to explain their twelve year old had refused to go to school and was threatening to run away. As I looked around the trashy place, I couldn't help but think I wouldn't have blamed him. I was then informed the son was in his bedroom down the hall and would not come out. The father said if I wanted, he would go kick the door in and drag the son out for me. I explained that wouldn't be necessary and I would rather talk to the child by myself.

I walked down the hallway and as I was about to knock on the door, I could hear the child crying on the other side. I knocked softly and asked the young fellow to open up. I heard the door unlock and was surprised to see a shirtless young boy standing in front of me. "Yes Sir?" He hardly looked out of control to me.

"What's this I hear about you not wanting to go to school?"

"No Sir, I'm not going."

"Why not?" I asked, "You not like school?"

"I love school Sir. I get to eat a good lunch and play with my friends."

"What kind of grades are you making?"

"I am on the Honor Roll."

"So, why all of a sudden do you not want to go to school?"

"I want to go, I just don't want to wear that shirt." With that the boy pointed to a purple striped shirt lying on top of a pile of obviously dirty laundry.

"What's wrong with your shirt that is keeping you from wanting to go to school?" I asked even though I could tell the shirt was obviously filthy.

The boy suddenly looked very adamant and stern, "Because I have worn it every day for a week, and the other kids are making fun of me saying I stink. They are calling me names and won't play with me."

"So if you had clean clothes, you would want to go to school?"

"Yes Sir, I've already missed part of they day."

"Have you eaten breakfast?" I asked, already knowing the answer.

"No Sir."

"How about I take you to school, we'll stop for a biscuit and I'll find a clean shirt for you somewhere along the way. Put your dirty shirt on for now and I'll take care of it."

The boy readily put his shirt on and grabbed a small Spiderman backpack from the floor. As we entered the living room, the father started yelling at the boy about getting his butt to school. I immediately told the father to be quiet and that I would be returning shortly to have a follow up conversation with them.

I loaded the boy in front seat of my cruiser and up the river we went towards the Detachment. I had dispatch contact Human Services and asked them to meet me at the Detachment. It didn't take long for me to realize why the other kids were making fun of this little fellow. To put it bluntly, he stunk pretty bad. I was forced to roll the four windows of my cruiser down just to be able to stand it.

Before we pulled into the Detachment, I went through McDonald's and got us a couple of biscuits and an orange juice. I left the boy in the break room eating his breakfast and asked the secretary to keep and eye on him as I walked down to Magic Mart and bought him two shirts. I also got him a stick of deodorant as he was obviously getting mature enough to need it.

Once I returned to the Detachment, Social Services was there and I quickly filled her in on what was going on. As we went back to the break room, I had the boy go to the bathroom to clean up and change shirts. I then explained the use of the deodorant and gave it to him. He looked fresh and was smiling when he came back into the break room, "Can I go to school now, please?"

As we dropped him off, I couldn't help but smile as he waved and ran to the door of the school. Now it was time to pay Mom and Dad a little visit.

Let's just say my conversation with the parents was not as pleasing to them as they would have liked. They were given twenty four hours to get the place cleaned up and then the Social Worker was going to make a return trip to inspect the house. I informed the two if the house was not clean then I would be returning to take custody of the child and file criminal charges against them.

When the Social Worker went back the next day she informed me the house was indeed a lot cleaner and the child's clothes had been washed.

I never saw the little boy again, but I did make several trips to the house after that with Social Services to ensure the parents were keeping the place clean. Each time I would go to the boy's room and ensure there were clean clothes for him to wear. I must say the parents did a decent turn around and did a better job of taking care of the kid, however it was a shame that it took an outside agency to force the parents to be actual parents. Several months later the family moved to the opposite end of the county and I never saw them again.

Sometimes the resiliency of a child would astonish me. There were a few instances when I felt like the child was trying to be strong so as to support the parent even though the child was the one who had suffered something terrible. There is one such child that I'll never forget.

One evening at the Detachment in Logan County, I was met with a lady who wished to make a complaint about her husband. Cindy explained she had remarried approximately three months prior and her new husband, Mike had moved in with her and her eleven year old daughter, Sarah. Shortly after the wedding, Sarah had started to act out against her new stepfather and began doing poorly in school. Sarah had always in the past been a straight A student, however now her grades had slid down considerably in a short period of time.

The previous evening Sarah had dropped the bomb and disclosed to her mother that Mike had been "massaging her legs" every day after school and recently had begun "massaging her inner thighs", occasionally slipping his fingers inside her panties.

Evidently, Mike, was unemployed and would meet Sarah as she got off the school bus everyday since Cindy did not get home from work for several more hours. At first it had been "massaging" with Sarah's pants on, eventually it progressed to "massages" without pants and recently Mike had progressed to actually rubbing her "bird", as Sarah called it.

All through the interview and investigation process, Sarah acted like a true Trooper. She told her story several times in the most matter of fact way, never wavering and never shedding the first tear. She was very descriptive and her details never changed. I remember looking at her one day and thinking, this little girl is aged way past her years.

On several occasions she stated she felt bad, because Mommy had lost her husband.

She also said she wanted to be strong so Mommy will not cry so much. Those comments always stuck in my mind as we moved through the whole process. Yet, never once did I even see a tear well up in her eyes as we moved closer to the looming trial date. She was without a doubt the toughest little girl I ever met.

Sarah did however have several requests for the trial. First, she did not want her mother in the courtroom when she was testifying. She said she did not want her mommy to have to listen to everything that had happened. She also wanted me to be the one to escort her from the witness room to the courtroom and then back afterward.

The case drew a lot of attention due to some crazy antics from Mike as the trial was about to start. The hallway outside of the courtroom was packed as the trial started and we moved through witness testimony. I testified and was cross examined first, Sarah would be last. Even though she had been rock solid for the months leading up to the trial, we still had concerns about how an eleven year old child would hold up to telling her story in front of Mike and the entire courtroom. This would be the first time she would be reciting the details with her stepfather in front of her.

We had made pretrial motions to have Sarah give her testimony remotely through CCTV citing several Supreme Court Cases in which the same thing had been done. The judge had ordered some psychiatric testing to see if she was competent to give witness testimony and be able to withstand the stress of doing it in front of Mike. The child blew through the testing and was deemed competent and able to give testimony in the court room. The judge ruled against us and stated the accused has the right to face his accuser. He did say the courtroom would be clear of all onlookers from the gallery leaving just the jury, attorneys, and the accused. Even though Sarah seemed comfortable, I wasn't.

On the morning Sarah was to begin testimony, the hallways of the courthouse were pretty crowded with family members and onlookers from both sides. All of the people who had been sitting in the courtroom all week were now hanging out in the hallway. The thing I didn't like, was I would have to lead Sarah through the crowd from the witness room to the courtroom.

When I went to get Sarah for her testimony, I couldn't help but think of how strong this little girl had been. I said a prayer asking God to just give her a little more strength to get through the next couple of hours. The part that concerned me the most was the defense attorney's cross examination questions. I knew the defense attorney from previous cases and knew he could be pretty harsh on witnesses, often pushing them to tears.

I opened the door to see Sarah coloring with Cindy seated beside her. There was also a family friend in the room with them. Sarah looked up and simply stated, "Is it my turn?"

"Yes, it is."

The look on Mom's face was one of pure anguish, however Sarah was as matter of fact as possible, "Ok, Mommy I'll be back in a little while. Love You."

With that, she walked over and grabbed my hand, "Let's go, Trooper Chris."

As I closed the door behind us, I could hear Cindy break down crying. Sarah never looked back. When we turned the corner and saw all of those people in the hallway, every eye was on us. Nobody said a word as we walked hand in hand through the crowd to the courtroom. Sarah never faltered, never missed a step, and never looked anywhere except straight ahead.

When we entered the courtroom, Sarah walked right over, sat in the chair and raised her hand. After the preliminary questions, that little girl spoke as clear as any adult and absolutely gave iron clad testimony sealing the fate of Mike. The more little Sarah talked, the lower Mike hung his head. Before long, he wouldn't even look at her or even in the direction of the witness stand. I could see tears in several of the jury members' eyes as Sarah talked about Mike putting his hand inside her panties and "massaging" her every day after school.

After she was finished, the defense attorney did not even put forth one cross examination question. He knew the more that little girl was on the witness stand speaking, the more likely his client was going to prison.

The judge then excused Sarah and gave me permission to take her back to the witness room. I took Sarah's hand and we exited the through the side door of the courtroom. We would have to turn two corners before we were back into the circus of all the onlookers.

I was so proud of Sarah, and quickly gave a prayer of Thanks to God for allowing her to make it through her part of the trial.

As the door shut behind us, we were briefly alone and suddenly Sarah stopped walking. "Trooper Chris is it all over?" she asked in a soft voice.

I could feel her little hand trembling slightly in my own hand, "Yes, it is completely over. You did really well."

She turned and started walking again, this time a little slower and looking at the floor. After a few steps, she stopped again. When she looked up at me, it was with the saddest eyes ever, "Trooper Chris, can I cry now?"

I knelt down, "Yes, Sweetheart, you are allowed to cry anytime you want."

The little girl, who had been so strong for all of us, suddenly came apart. She wrapped her arms around my neck and we both cried. I carried her back to the witness room with my head high and tears in my eyes. She kept her face buried in my shoulder as months of held back tears poured out uncontrollably. Nobody said a word as I walked through that crowd of people. The Big Trooper with tears in his eyes and a crying little girl in his arms. I think if one person had uttered a sound I would have completely ripped their head off. I was not going to let anything be said to or about her as we took the walk back to her mother.

When I returned to the courtroom, I remember looking at the shoulder of my uniform and seeing Sarah's tears were still wet on it. I was elated to learn that the defense attorney wanted to stop the trial and negotiate a guilty plea. Sarah's testimony had been that strong.

When it was all over with, Mike was going to do ten years in prison for giving his "massages". Cindy ended up eventually remarrying several years later and the last I heard had moved out of state. Little Sarah seemed to recover pretty well through counseling and her grades were soon back to normal.

My hope is Sarah has grown to be a wonderful young lady and has a family of her own. You always wish the best for the victims, however that innocence God gave them at birth has forever been taken away. Quite frequently the victimized children grow up to be offenders themselves. No amount of counseling can give back what a pedophile all too often takes away.

Me? I was tired. I was proud of being able to get the prison time we got for Mike, however seeing the look in that little girl's eyes right before she broke down will forever be with me. I have no doubt she had been holding back all of her emotions, hurt, and pain for the benefit of her mother. She stated several times she felt bad for her mother losing her husband because of her telling what happened.

That afternoon after the trial wrapped up, I went straight home and grabbed each of my children and hugged them tight. I thanked God for each of them and their innocence as I held them close. They couldn't understand why I had tears in my eyes as I told them over and over that I loved them.

After the trial of Mike, I tried not to take on so many child abuse cases. The emotional toll had added up. I needed a break from them for a while. I think if ever there was a time in my life I would have become an alcoholic, it would have been then. Without the kids and God I probably would have.

You see, we all have to deal with the built up emotion in one way or another. Some deal with it in a positive manner, others in a self destructive manner. All too often, officers, whether they are male or female, are not considered manly or strong enough to be officers by their peers or superiors if they show emotion. So, some keep it bottled up inside where it boils and festers into something bad.

I dealt with my anger and emotions in the weight room. I pounded the weights as hard as I could in order to vent most of my frustrations. Frustrations over the suspects, the slow court systems, the lack of sleep, lack of time with my family, you name it.

At that time, I was very fortunate to have a wonderful Pastor in my life who I could talk to and pray with. There were times I would go to see him during the week and we would pray together. Often we would pray for strength and healing for the victims I had dealt with. Pastor Steve is a wonderful man and helped me more than he will ever know. I am forever in his debt for listening to me and for his prayers.

To the countless victims I have been involved with over the years, I prayed for you then and I continue to pray for you even now. Even though I can not remember each of your names, I remember each of your faces. I also remember the pain each of you suffered and the innocence you lost. I would have done anything to take away the pain and let you enjoy being a kid again.

Unfortunately, I am not able to do that….

In that I feel my own guilt and pain.,,,

Walking Through the Valley of the Shadow of Death….

Death….

Every Law Enforcement Officer deals with it on an almost daily basis. Like fingerprints, no two deaths are the same, as such the way we deal with each death is different. Some of us are better than others at dealing with the circumstances surrounding these emotional scenes. It's impossible to pick up the lifeless body of an infant or child and not think of your own. There was more than one instance in which I drove home as fast as I could at the end of my shift, just to give my family a hug, or if I was working late shift, look in their bedrooms and listen intently for the sound of their breathing as they slept.

When I worked for the Sheriff's Department, this was an unexpected emotional difficulty. I was working in the County my family was raised in, as such, often times I would find myself dealing with working the scene of someone I was acquainted with, a friend of, or even related to. Sometimes it may have been a petty crime, a fatal accident, or a major crime scene.

At that time I had a lot of friends in the County, and often times if I had a few spare minutes I would pull off to the side of the road and talk to them in front of their house. One such family was on my way home, as their son played football with my son, I frequently saw them outside my job. I always had my dog, Blue, with me and often I would let the kids look at him through the window. Sometimes I would get out and visit for a few minutes.

One day I was one of the responding officers to a fatal accident, unfortunately one of the occupants turned out to be the son of my friends who played ball with my son. He had been riding with his grandfather, who had lost control of his truck and crashed into a power pole. It was one of the hardest things I had ever experienced, trying to maintain my professional composure as I helped work the scene. Afterwards, I felt like I needed to be the one to inform the family of this life altering tragedy.

The boy had only been eight years old, one year younger than my own son. I had seen this child at the elementary school when I had done different activities and dog demonstrations with the students. I had watched him run across the football field loving the game. I had been to his house and was friends with his family. This was a struggle.

After a brief drive I arrived at his house, his mother was working in the front yard and waved as I pulled in the driveway. As I got out of my vehicle, I put my campaign hat on and instantly the mother began to scream and cry. I was briefly confused as I had not even said a word to her yet. However, she collapsed, crying in a heap in the front yard. I rushed over to console her, she looked at me and said, "Just tell me, is he dead?"

I softly said, "Yes, I'm sorry. He is." We both cried in the front yard together.

There was just one thing that I could never figure out, and did not have the opportunity to inquire about until about a year later at a school basketball game when I saw the mother. I knew it was going to drag up some emotional feelings, but I had to ask her. How did she know without me saying a word what had happened?

"Well," she replied, "you have been to our house before in uniform and there have been times you have gotten out of your car. However, of all the times you have visited us, you never got out and immediately put your hat on. When you did that, I knew what had happened. The rest of my family was safely inside the house, it had to be my son." Again, we both cried together.

Quite frequently, it's not the dead that bother you the most, but the living. Delivering death messages is an aspect of the job, very few discuss. In my opinion, we don't do enough to prepare our young officers in the emotional roller coaster of death and the living. Nor do we do enough for our experienced officers in handling the after math of the devastation. All too often, the officer is left to their own devices in dealing with the care of their mental well beings. This is the main reason most officers can be said to have a twisted sense of humor. It's not because we actually find the situation funny, but because the laughter or chuckle is a coping mechanism we often have to employ to fight back our emotions.

My first experience delivering a message of death came one day early in my career at the Sheriff's Department. I walked into the Department one morning, only to have the Sheriff call me into his office. As I entered, the Sheriff told me a lady had been killed in a vehicle accident in the northern part of the state. Somebody needed to drive out to the family farm and inform her husband of thirty four years, his wife was dead.

At first I was floored, until that point I had never thought of having to tell a complete stranger their life long love was dead. That was a part of the job movies never glorified or television ever highlighted. I got the information from the Sheriff and headed out to deliver my grim news to an unsuspecting citizen.

When I turned up the farmer's long dirt driveway, I couldn't help but be nervous. I looked and there was an older gentlemen coming out of the house and walking to meet me at the end of the drive. The old fellow was very polite and offered his hand while introducing himself. Sure enough, this was the person I was looking for.

As soon as I said, "Sir, I regret to inform you," the look on his face went from pleasant to one of extreme anguish. I don't think he heard much past those words. He never shed a single tear in front of me, but you could tell he was struggling to maintain his composure. I offered to stay with him until some family members got there, but he would have none of that. He told me thank you, and walked back to the house alone.

I got back in my cruiser and left, driving with a million things on my mind. The old guy had handled it better than I thought I would have. I could only imagine how he felt.

See, law enforcement is one of the most emotional professions in the world. And it's not always your own emotions, but those around you. Emotions will always breed similar emotions. We, as humans, will always feed off the feelings of others, no matter if the emotions are good or bad. It's in our makeup, we can't help it.

So when you deliver a life altering message such as a death notice, you will almost always soak up some of the anguish felt by the loved ones. After a while, negative emotions will pile up, if you don't a way to bleed off the built up pressure.

As we, the public servant, each deal with the death differently, so do the survivors. We always think the bereaved will just automatically fall to pieces crying. Sometimes, this is far from the case. I once knocked on a man's door at two in the morning to inform him his brother had just been stabbed to death in a fight. As I knocked on the door, I could hear people running through the house, however nobody would answer the door. I then heard a loud, whisper on the other side of the door exclaim, "It's the Law, what have you done now?"

"Nothing this time, I swear!" came the reply.

I again knocked stating that nobody was going to jail, I just needed to talk to them. The talking inside quieted and the door cracked. "You are telling the truth? I ain't going to jail this time?"

"Not this time, probably next time, but not this time." With that said the man opened the door the rest of the way and I could see his wife standing behind him in the dark. After confirming he was the deceased's brother, I then informed him of his sibling's demise.

Needless to say I was quite stunned when he started chuckling and then laughing hysterically, "Is that all?"

"Uh, yes. Can you give me the correct address of your mother, or would you prefer to tell her?"

"Mom? I see her about every three or four days, I'll try to remember to give her the news the next time I see her."

The man never stopped laughing as his wife broke down crying. I finally convinced him to give me Mom's information so I could inform her also. Once I found her, she, on the other hand, broke down miserably.

A small post script to that story, yes, the next time I saw the man, I did in fact have to arrest him. I caught him driving intoxicated several months later. As soon as I approached the driver's window and he realized it was me, he again started laughing.

"You told me you were going to arrest me the next time you saw me. I guess you were right, because I'm drunk as hell and my license is suspended!"

Each time I delivered a death notice, I felt some of the pain of the loss. Sometimes I felt a little, other times it would hit me much harder. One lady in Logan County I will never forget, she hit me with an emotional sledge hammer.

I got a call one afternoon to Logan General Hospital for a drug overdose death. Upon my arrival at the Emergency Room, the charge nurse informed a family had brought in their thirty five year old son after finding him in his bedroom unresponsive. She told me he had been Dead on Arrival and the death appeared to possibly be from a collection of empty pill bottles lying on the bed with him when he was found. She continued to tell me the room number he was currently laying and members of the family were still there with the deceased. As I thanked her and turned to go to the room, she stated, "Um, Trooper, just so you know, the mother seems to be having a rough time with it." I again thanked her and headed to continue my investigation.

As I entered the hospital room I was taken aback with what I was met. Beside the bed was the father quietly crying along with several other people. Sitting beside the bed was the mother holding the hand of the deceased patting it. "Shhhhhhh, he's sleeping. He's not feeling well and just dozed off. Please don't wake him yet Trooper," said the mother. As I looked, I noticed the hospital had started an IV line in the same arm the lady was patting the hand of. The site of the injection had bled slightly and the woman had her son's blood on her hands, but was oblivious to the fact.

The father then moved from behind the bed and asked me to step outside. He informed me his wife was refusing to accept her son's death and she kept saying he would be waking up soon. During the conversation, I informed him to bring his wife to the Detachment as soon as possible so I could collect statements from them. The man agreed to meet me as soon as he could get his wife to leave.

A short time later, I was standing behind the counter of the Detachment as the man and his wife entered. I started to express my sorrow for their loss when the lady interrupted me saying, "Trooper, can we please hurry up with this? My son will be waking up soon and I want to be there when he does."

I looked at the father who just shrugged his shoulders and began to cry again. I then noticed the lady still had her son's blood on her hands. "Ma'am, if you like, you are more than welcome to wash your hands in the rest room right there."

The lady looked at her hands as if she was noticing the blood for the first time. She stared in disbelief for an uncomfortable period of time, turning her hands and looking at them. She then noticed a small amount of blood on her shirt, looking at me with a huge sense of realization, she simply stated in a quiet voice, "He's not going to wake up, is he?"

"No Maam, he's not"

With that, the mother collapsed upon the floor in total anguish as her husband attempted to calm her. As I turned, so the family would not see the tears in my eyes, I caught the gaze of the dispatcher working in the next room, who also was trying to calm her crying eyes.

I will never forget the look in that lady's eyes. Even though I can not remember her name, her face will forever haunt me. I had never seen such a mix of confusion and loss and have not since.

I hope I never have to again.

Suicide and the "Why"

Suicide….

No single word can impact a family more than this single word. A fatality in an automobile wreck or even a murder is extremely traumatizing to everyone. However, there is one thing suicide leaves behind more than the others….Unanswered questions. Yes, there are often unanswered questions in these other events, but none as much as taking ones own life.

In suicide there is always the big question of, "Why? Why did this happen? Why didn't they talk to me? Why did they do this? They seemed so at peace lately, I thought everything was getting better."

A whole bunch of "Why" questions, questions that most of the time never get answered. There is only one person that can truly answer them and that person is no longer with the living.

Wait a minute, what about the note? Surely they left the remaining family a note. I'm positive everything will be answered in that magical little piece of paper. "Where is it,

Trooper? Please let me have it so all of my questions will be answered!"

"I'm sorry, there was no mess age left behind."

"You're not telling me the truth! My brother would not have done this without leaving something behind! Give it to me!"

I have had similar conversations like this quite a few times over the years. In the suicides I have been involved with, very few times is there anything left behind other than heart broken family members and non believing friends. On several occasions, I have been accused of hiding the suicide note for one conspiracy theory or another. My estimate is in at least ninety five percent of the suicides I worked, there was no message of any kind left behind.

Delivering suicide death messages to relatives was what I disliked the most. I knew I was going to get that one word question, "Why?" The one question, that I had no way of answering.

When I first started wanting a career in law enforcement there was always a huge concern I had, my first suicide call. How would I react? How would I be affected emotionally? How would I handle dealing with the family? And most importantly, could I recover and perform my job in the professional manner I knew I would have to?

You see, I too have asked that question, "Why?".

It was 13 December, 1981, I was thirteen years old and lying on my bed watching the Dallas Cowboys play the Philadelphia Eagles. I was wearing my Dallas 33 jersey and hoping the Cowboys could hold off the Eagles as the fourth quarter was winding down.

Suddenly, my mother called me to the dining room, where she was sitting with my aunt. As I entered, my mother looked at me very matter of fact and said, "Chris, your Dad shot himself earlier today."

My parents had divorced when I was four years old and my father had been living out of state since. I had not been able to see him after he moved out. I had been able to talk to him on the phone once several years earlier and that had pretty much been the extent of my contact with him. As a small boy, I often dreamed and wished I could see him. Now I would never get that chance.

I felt numb. I remember just standing there and staring at my mother and aunt.

"Do you have any questions?" asked mom.

"Why?"

"Nobody knows."

I just turned and walked back to my room, the game was over, the Cowboys had won but I didn't care. I laid on my bed and just stared at the wall. All of my dreams, wishing, and praying had been for nothing. I would never know my father.

"Why?"

It's now thirty five years later, and I'm still asking that question.

When I was sixteen years old, a childhood friend of mine went home from school one day to find his father on his knees in the kitchen with his head in the oven. He too asked the "Why" questions for years. There were several times he and I would talk about the suicides of our fathers. He and I had known each other since kindergarten and had always been good friends.

However, it did not take long for me to realize we were definitely dealing with the deaths of our fathers in very different ways. I tended to be very quiet about my father's suicide and kept it closed within myself. I hated to talk about and still do. Even today, there are going to be a lot of people who read this and will be surprised because they never knew how I lost my dad.

It has been hard to open up about it while writing this manuscript. Even now, I sit here typing with tears in my eyes.

"Why?"

No answer.

My friend was beginning to act out and do very poorly in school. He ended up being held back a year and did not graduate with the rest of his friends. I think this just compounded the emotional things he was struggling with. When his father had passed, he inherited a decent amount of money from the sale of their house and a life insurance policy. He went on huge spending sprees and it did not take long before he was pretty much broke.

After I left for the military I lost track of him and often wondered if he had ever been able to fully cope with the loss of his father and recover from it.

When I was hired by the Sheriff's Department, it didn't take long for that first suicide call to come in. I was working day shift and it was getting close to time to head home. I had just walked into the office when the Chief Deputy yelled at me, "Hey, let's go, there's a suicide in the middle of Coal River Road!"

Away we went, he in his cruiser and me following behind in mine. It was about twenty minutes of hard driving. A long twenty minutes. Along the way, we actually drove past my house. The kids were outside playing and stopped to wave as we blew past with our sirens wailing.

I couldn't help but be nervous as we got closer to the scene. This would be my first suicide call. I was determined that I would be professional and do my job with a stern face. Nothing could prepare me for what I saw when we got there.

The information we got was a man and woman had been driving on a small country road on the north county line. The woman was driving as an argument broke out between the two. She pulled to the side of the road as her husband got out of the vehicle and walked around to her side. Standing outside the driver's door, the man pulled a .357 magnum from his pants, shot himself in the head, and was currently lying dead in the middle of the road.

As we pulled up on the scene, I could see a maroon minivan sitting to the side of the road. As I got out of my cruiser, and walked closer to the scene, I saw it. A brain, a complete brain looking as I had studied it in text books, lying in the middle of the road. It was sitting there as if someone had just set it down on the pavement.

Then I saw him, he was lying in the road flat on his back with a handgun still in his hand. The guy looked as if he was taking a nap with his brain lying beside him and a neat little hole in his temple. It was my father, I was seeing my father lying there in the middle of the road.

I stopped for a brief second and just stared at my dad. As I walked around the body, I noticed he was missing the entire other side of his head. It was literally splattered all over the side of the van. The man's wife was sitting on the side of the road crying. I looked at her and realized her face was covered with his blood and skull fragments.

I've got to do this, I thought. This is the call I've been waiting for. Time to get busy and prove to myself I can do this. I quickly asked the Chief what he wanted me to do and busied myself in the tasks he gave me. It took us about an hour to get everything wrapped up and the body sent to the Medical Examiner's Office.

I got in my cruiser and slowly drove toward home. Suddenly, I realized I couldn't go home yet. I had the most overwhelming need to go to the cemetery. My father was buried close to my house and there was no way I could go home without going there first. I don't know why, but the need to see my father's grave was almost suffocating, it was that strong.

A few minutes later I pulled into the tiny cemetery and drove to the back corner where I could see his stone. I got out of my cruiser and put my campaign hat on as I slowly walked to the foot of his grave. His marker is one given to Veterans for their service to our country. Charles Ray Holbert, Vietnam, I read the writing. I snapped to attention and smartly saluted him, and then my emotions overwhelmed me. I dropped to one knee with tears pouring out of my eyes and asked the question, "Why?".

Still, no answer.

I did however feel a sense of relief. For a while I had been wondering how I would react, how I would perform. I had been able to keep a professional attitude and do my duty, I was proud of that fact. I had been able to present that look of confidence at a time that I wasn't actually all too confident.

After that day, I found I wasn't as nervous when I would get those calls of a suicide. And I never did see my dad's face anymore after working that first scene. Even though I never did get completely comfortable working them, I always did my best when I got the calls.

As a matter of fact, the last call I responded to as a Deputy ended up being an attempted suicide. I was on my way home when I got the call to meet a lady at a small country gas station to make a report of a domestic dispute. I arrived at the tiny store and was met by a lady in hospital scrubs with tears rolling down her face.

She was quick to tell of an argument with her husband that had quickly turned violent when she came home from work. She then stated she had left as he started to throw items across the home. I told her to wait there as I was going to the house to get his side of the story.

I drove the short distance to their country home and could see a red Ford Ranger truck sitting in the driveway with the passenger door standing open as I pulled in. I then saw the lady's husband at the door of the house with his back to me as if he were locking the door. I was approximately twenty yards away as I looked into the truck and saw an arsenal of long guns and hand guns sitting in the passenger seat.

My hand instantly went to my gun as I jumped out of the cruiser. The man turned to look at me and I immediately saw the black gun in his right hand. I raised my service weapon, then everything slowed down. Front sight, center mass, I kept thinking as I saw him turn to face me and his gun rising up.

Front sight, center mass, as I looked through my rear sights to let the front sight come to rest on his sternum.

I yelled for him to drop the gun, as my brain again said front sight, center mass. All of those drills on the Academy firing range were coming in to play as muscle memory took over.

All I saw now was the single green dot of my front glow in the dark night sight as I felt the slack come out of my Smith and Wesson 4006 trigger. I knew there was a shiny copper jacketed hollow point inside the chamber waiting for me to complete the trigger pull.

His gun was almost level, time slowed even more. He was shouting something at me but my body had shut my hearing down as it now funneled all blood and energy to the important body functions required for survival. I couldn't hear a thing except for the words front sight, center mass over and over in my head.

I felt the hard pull of the trigger as I knew the hammer of my gun was on its backward journey from the double action of the weapon.

His gun was chest high as he suddenly turned the barrel onto the center of his own chest and pulled the trigger. He shot himself right in front of me. I released the tension on my trigger and watched the hammer come back to rest.

The man was down on the porch and I could suddenly hear him moaning loudly as I approached and my hearing started to come back. His gun had fallen off the porch as he dropped to the floor. When I got to him, I holstered my gun and quickly searched him; I then got on the radio and called for some assistance and an ambulance.

As I started to give the man first aid, I started to get angry, really angry. Who was this idiot to force me to almost shoot him? Who was he to put such a decision on me? The more he laid on the porch and cried, the more I wanted to punch him in the face for putting me through the stress I had just experienced.

He had a small hole in the middle of his chest. I could see where the bullet had struck his sternum and ricocheted downward into his abdomen. I could see a slight bulge of tissue at the bottom edge of the bone. The more the man squirmed, the bigger the bulge became. Finally without warning a foot long section of small intestine came squirting out of the hole. It looked like a big fat piece of sausage as it lay on his chest.

I noticed his eyes got pretty large as he looked at his own guts protruding out of his chest. "That don't look good," he said.

I just looked at him, shook my head, and said, "No, it sure doesn't."

The ambulance was about twenty minutes out, so I had some time trying to keep the man calm and from dropping too far into shock. The closest responding Deputy was also about thirty minutes out. I had retrieved my first aid bag from the trunk of the cruiser and gently wrapped the piece of intestine in gauze and wet it with some saline solution. I tried to keep the man's focus on me instead of the gray colored sausage on his chest.

At one point he looked at me and said, "I didn't think it would hurt this bad."

Really, are you serious? He didn't think it would hurt this bad? Sure, a .40 caliber hollow point bullet to the chest should be a pleasant experience.

Once the ambulance got there, we got him quickly on the gurney and loaded into the back. Now that I had him off my hands and another Deputy there, I had time to take a closer look at everything.

The man had loaded every weapon he could find into the front seat of his truck along with copious amounts of ammunition. Whenever I had asked him where he was going when I arrived, he would only say he had wanted to talk to his wife and he was going to find her. Lucky for her, I got to the house first.

As it was only a couple of weeks before Christmas, I noticed the family tree was resting in the nearby creek along with quite a few decorations and wrapped gifts. As I went through the house, I looked at the family portraits and saw that each picture had been removed and the man's face cut out, placed back in the frame, and hung back on the wall. When I entered the dining room, I found an ashtray with the cut out faces and a shredded marriage certificate.

After about an hour, the scene was wrapped up and the ambulance was on its way to the hospital. Then I remembered his wife. I drove back to the gas station and sure enough she was still sitting there with tears on her face.

I relayed to her what had happened and gave her the hospital information, then it came.

"Why?"

"I don't know Ma'am."

People outside of the military and law enforcement don't realize the stress of putting a gun sight on another human's chest and taking the slack out of the trigger as you get ready to drop the hammer. It's a whole different level and type of stress and emotion.

I remember always hearing people say, "I could shoot somebody without any regrets or problems."

To those, I say, you have no clue. You have no idea if you can actually go through with it until the hammer is about to fall. It's not like you see on television, it never is.

One day I was at the Medical Examiner's Office for an autopsy of a case I was working. As we wrapped up, I walked out of the examination room, began to remove my protective garments and get cleaned up. One of the ME's assistants came up the hallway pushing a gurney with a body on it as they prepared for the next examination.

"You guys sure are busy today," I said.

"Yea, Mondays always are," she replied. "Hey, you're a South Charleston Boy, aren't you?"

"I graduated with the class of 1986."

"Well, you probably know this one, he's from South Charleston and you're the same age. This guy put a garden hose from his car's exhaust pipe to the inside of the car and killed himself."

I walked over and looked at the tag on the body bag, it was my child hood friend. The same friend I had grown up with, the same one I had been a Boy Scout with, played ball with, and shared the loss of our fathers with.

I was stunned. I never expected to walk into the Medical Examiner's Office and see a child hood friend lying on a gurney.

"The note he left sure started out in a weird way."

"Huh, note? There was a note?"

"Yes, it said he always knew he would end up this way."

I left without saying much else. I had a million thoughts going through my head as I drove home. Soon my phone started blowing up with everybody calling about our friend's death. It didn't take long for me to turn my phone off as I sat on the back deck by myself deep in thought.

He always knew he would end up this way.

My heart ached for my lost friend and even more for the children he had left behind.

He always knew he would end up this way, the words kept revolving in my head.

I am the exact opposite. I know I can never end up that way. It has now been thirty five years since the day I lost my father and it hurts just as much now as it ever did back then. Almost every day I ask "Why?" I now understand the unanswered questions and the unending hurt. I also understand I would never want to put that hurt and pain on my family.

I have studied suicide a lot over the years, and my friend proved one statistic that I have come across many times. A large percentage of children who lose a parent to suicide often commit the deed themselves.

I am determined not to be another statistic, to break the chain, to never pass this pain and unending stream of unanswered questions to my children. I will suffer lifelong agony to save my children the pain of what I have had to endure. My children will never ask the "Why" questions.

Dealing with the suicide of an unknown person is one thing, dealing with the suicide of a brother Trooper was not something I was ready for. Actually, none of us were ready for it. It was one of the worst days I ever had in law enforcement. A day I will never forget.

I walked into the Detachment that morning, like any other morning, and the Secretary hit me with it.

"Did you hear what happened last night?"

"No, what's up?

She then dropped a bomb and told me of a fellow Trooper at another Detachment that had shot himself. Evidently he had been sitting in the driveway of his house, in his cruiser, in uniform. He had pulled his service weapon, put it in his own ribcage, and pulled the trigger.

"Why?" I asked.

The Trooper was the kind of guy you couldn't help but like. I had worked with him on several occasions over the years on different details and cases. I remembered him as being joyful and laughing with him a lot. I knew he lived relatively close to me and had a wife and several kids.

Even though I did not work with him every day, it still hit hard because he was a Brother Trooper. Someone who wore the same uniform and badge that I did. In the days that followed there so many rumors and accusations flying around that nobody knew what was fact or fiction. I got to the point where I didn't want to hear anything else about it. All I can say for certain is, attending his funeral was a very hard thing to do.

As I spoke with other Troopers, everybody was having a hard time with it. Nobody could understand why it happened or how to handle it.

At that time our Department did not have any kind of grief counseling or outreach program. As Troopers, we did not have anybody to talk to except each other. There was nowhere to deal with the emotions and sorrow of losing one of our own.

The one good thing to come of the whole mess, was going forward, we were offered free anonymous personal and marriage counseling. It was at least a step in the right direction.

All too often law enforcement officers have no options for relief of their stress. Work stress compounded with the at home stress is a bad combination. One feeds off the other and makes both that much harder to deal with sometimes.

In training at the different academies across the country, we do a great job of preparing new officers for the physical rigors and demands of the job. However, I feel law enforcement as a whole does a poor job of preparing these same people for the mental stress of life wearing a badge and gun. It is an awesome responsibility one is given when the badge is pinned to their chest and they are sworn to Serve and Protect.

Think about it, how many people outside the military go to work every day with the ability, training, and authority to take a life in certain situations? It is a responsibility that should garner the utmost respect and be placed in the best trained individuals both physically and mentally.

It's time we give our law enforcement the total package of support they deserve and more than anything, each have earned.

To my fallen Brother I say....

"Rest easy, I hope you found peace. We Love and Miss You."

The Families

When you walk the path of a law enforcement officer, you will experience days filled with aggravation and stress. There will be days you see atrocities others can only imagine in their worse dreams. These things can and will add up like a huge weight pressing down on you. With all of that emotion and stress, it's impossible to leave it all behind and not bring those feelings home with you.

It's hard for your family to understand there are things you feel like you need to discuss. While some days you just need to be left alone for a few minutes in an opportunity to decompress.

This lack of understanding can all too often add pressure to any family situation. You can't blame the family, they don't realize what you may have seen or experienced that day. You can't blame the officer because he or she is trying to spare the family the details of the blood and violence.

So it's all too often the stress and emotions are felt by the entire family and not just the officer who was actually at the scene. It's very hard to explain to a child why you had to miss a birthday party because somebody committed suicide.

To a little boy, he thinks you were not there because you didn't want to see him blow out his candles. While you would have given anything to be there, in law enforcement, you can't just up and go home at quitting time. If you are involved with a scene or investigation, you can't leave for home until it's completed.

One time I went to work on Wednesday afternoon and did not return home until almost Saturday morning. I was still wearing the same clothes on Friday that I had put on two days earlier. During that time I missed a big family dinner. I wanted to be there, however I had spent the last several days running hard on a murder case where a young lady had been burned alive after being stuffed into the trunk of her car.

Even though my family had nothing to do with the investigation, they still felt the pain of me not being home. And they couldn't help but feel like I wasn't home because I would rather be somewhere else. I would have rather been home reading stories to my little girls or fishing off the bridge with my boy, but my sense of duty and dedication kept me away. It sure wasn't because I didn't love them. I love those children with every once of my being.

The Good Lord blessed me with some of the best children I could ever hope for, making me an extremely proud father. They have truly been the best thing that ever happened to me. Of all the titles I have earned over the years, the one I cherish the most is "Daddy." There is no greater feeling in the world than the love of your children.

Looking back, I just wish I could have done a better job of being a father.

Not saying that I feel like I've been a bad father, however I hated missing out on as much as I did. Due to either being gone for training or working crazy hours for years, there were a lot of events in my kid's lives I wish I could have attended. To this day I harbor a lot of guilt over having missed so much. There was one stretch where I worked five Christmas Holidays in a row due to being on shift. Not exactly the ideal family Christmas, when daddy has to leave as soon as the presents have been opened to go to work.

Pretty much my whole adult life has been spent in a uniform in the service of others, which I do not regret at all. I feel nothing but pride for the service I have given to God, Family, Country, and State. I would proudly do it again in a heartbeat. I have considered it nothing but a true privilege that God allowed me to be a servant to my fellow man.

Ever since I was a teenager I had a desire to serve in the military. I am proud to be from a family with a tradition of serving this wonderful country. Two of my most cherished possessions are the American flags that draped my grandfather's and my father's caskets at the time of their funerals. Flags they received for their military service, and one day my son will receive those flags along with my own.

When I was in the military, we did not have the communication abilities that military personnel have today. We did not have internet or Skype. It was snail mail and maybe a long distance phone call in some foreign country after waiting a couple of hours in line for my turn to use the one pay phone.

I did two, six month long deployments during the seven years of my military career and countless shorter trips to foreign lands and other states. Each time I was forced to leave a small, beautiful little girl behind. It was like a knife in the stomach every time I deployed. Each day was spent looking forward to when I could come home again to see her, to hold her, and more than anything, hear that sweet little voice tell me she loved me. Every time we returned, I would try my best to find her in the crowd waiting on the pier. Each time, I would be amazed at how quick she was growing. And then, before long, it was time for Daddy to leave again. But, she was always there when I returned, squealing and running to meet me, jumping in my arms with tears in my eyes.

After the military, I was again forced away from my family each time I went to the West Virginia State Police Academy. This time there was the addition of my son and a set of beautiful twin girls. Every Sunday afternoon that I had to go back to the Academy was absolutely gut wrenching.

When I was in the Academy for the Sheriff's Department, my son was only three years old. Every Sunday afternoon as I waited for my ride to pick me up, you could feel the tension as everybody prepared for me to leave. When the other deputy arrived to pick me up, there would be hugs and tears as I walked out the door.

One Sunday toward the end of the Sixteen week Academy class, my son would not come to give me a hug good bye. The little three year old boy looked at my partner with a stern face and said, "I hate you." This was a complete surprise as my son had always enjoyed him being there before.

"Why would you say that?" I asked.

"Because he takes my Daddy away!" pouted my little fellow.

My heart broke into a million pieces. It wasn't my partner's fault I had to leave, it was part of the training. However, my son was too young to understand my going away. All he knew was every time my buddy came to the house, Daddy had to leave for a week. I hugged my little boy with tears in my eyes and tried to explain to him why I had to leave. That was the closest I ever came to quitting the Academy.

Those children have truly made more sacrifices than I ever did. I had a choice, however, they did not. I have had a lot of people me thank me for my service over the years, but I don't think I have ever truly told my children "Thank You". I can only hope those little blessed hearts know how much their Daddy truly missed them. How much he loves them, and how proud he is for the sacrifices they made without complaint. They gave me their love and support to me regardless of the situation.

I can remember on multiple occasions, I would pull into the driveway at the end of my shift and see the kids running to me. Then, as I would try to mark off duty with the county dispatch, I would get the grim news that my shift was in fact not over like I thought. Instead of giving Daddy-is-home-for-dinner hugs, I would have to give Daddy-is-leaving hugs and pull right back out of the driveway.

When you work for a small rural Sheriff's Department or a smaller State Police Detachment, you don't always have the luxury of somebody coming on shift behind you. So if there's a call, mental hygiene, or any other kind of emergency you have to take it.

It's very disheartening when you know there is dinner on the table waiting for you and you have to leave it and your family behind. I have eaten many leftovers out of the microwave oven because of this very thing.

While those who have made sacrifices in the service of our God, Country, and Fellow Man deserve recognition, the true heroes are the families left behind. They are the ones who truly sacrifice their loved one, so he or she may serve somewhere else. They are the ones who must do without so others may reap the benefits of that individual's service. They are also the ones left behind to hear and deal with the negativity of that loved one's efforts to make this a better world for all people.

The stress of missing five Christmas Holidays in a row was not felt by just me, but the entire family. Every birthday I missed not only broke my heart, but that of a small child also. Every school play or function missed just added that much more stress to an already hard situation.

So the next time you tell a soldier, police, fire, or EMS person "Thanks for your service", don't forget the same courtesy to the family standing beside him or her supporting their efforts. Don't forget without the loving and patient family support, that person would not be able serve and protect on a daily basis.

The following is a little poem given to me by my oldest daughter the day I graduated from the Academy for the Lincoln County Sheriff's Department. She was ten years old at the time….

My Dad's A Deputy
My Dad's a Deputy and I'm Proud of him
My Dad's a Deputy
And he makes a difference.
My Dad's a Deputy

And I feel safe at night.
My Dad's a deputy
And I Love Him.
If he never comes home
He's doing his job in Heaven….

To my children, I Thank You. I thank you for every one of your sacrifices so that I was able to fulfill my destiny to serve others. Thank you so much for your patience and support of me as I went forth to make the world a little better place. Words can not express the pride and love I have for you….

Nor can words express the guilt I feel for having missed so much….

I'm sorry you did not have a choice….

Fallen Brothers

In the writing of these thoughts, I can't help but think about all of the great men and women I have truly been honored to toe the line with. And I also can't help but think about the ones who have fallen along the way.

When I started making a list of ones I have called Brother and Friend, I was taken back by the sheer number of friends who were either injured or killed in the line of duty during my time as a Deputy and Trooper. Don't get me wrong, it wasn't that I didn't know beforehand the number was high. I just didn't exactly realize it was that high.

When I graduated from the Academy for the Sheriff's department, it didn't take long before the first one fell. It had only been four weeks since graduation when I got the phone call one evening. One of our classmates had been transporting a prisoner back to West Virginia from Pennsylvania, traveling south on the interstate. Another vehicle got on the wrong ramp and entered the south bound lane going north. As the entering vehicle topped the ramp, the two collided. Our classmate died at the scene.

Several months later, another of our class was also killed in a motor vehicle accident. I remember standing at attention outside of the funeral home in a detail of officers from around the state. I started thinking, "Is this what law enforcement is about? Going from one funeral to the next for your Brothers and Sisters?" We had lost two class members in a matter of several months, I couldn't help but wonder how many more would we lose? Was I to be one of them?

Going to the funeral of a fallen law enforcement officer is a different kind of experience. To begin with, I am not someone who does well at funerals since the loss of my father. But the funeral of a fellow officer is especially tough for me.

When the city of Charleston lost an officer several years ago, I was standing outside of the Civic Center at attention in formation waiting to enter, and was struck by the silence. We were in the middle of the capital city on a weekday afternoon and nobody was saying a word. The roads had been closed to traffic, and even though there were hundreds of people in a group, you could hear nothing but the chirping of birds. It was as if the entire city was taking a few moments to honor the fallen public servant.

The hardest thing for me is when they do Last Call of the officer's unit number over the radio. There is a speaker hooked to the county dispatch radio for everyone to hear at the service. At the appointed time, everybody is silent as the dispatcher calls roll of all officers on duty. Every unit on duty can be heard answering roll until the unit number for the fallen member is called, there is nothing but silence. The unit number is called again, only silence again. Then the dispatcher will mark the unanswered unit number as permanently off duty. It is absolutely gut wrenching. I hate the silence of Last Call, it's like the final confirmation that particular unit number will never again be answered.

Then the bagpipes start. To this day, the sound of Amazing Grace on bagpipes easily breaks down my emotions. I will always associate the song with the death of an officer, it's hard to hear sometimes, even in church.

I have had seven friends shot, and three of those have died. Four officers I knew died from injuries associated with a vehicle accident, while quite a few others have been seriously injured. Another five were injured from being struck by a vehicle, two of those were intentional strikes. One friend died from a heart attack while training students at the Academy. An additional four have been lost by suicide.

I am unable to even begin to count the number of Brothers and Sisters that have been injured in one way or another in the line of duty. I have seen injuries of all types, everything from vehicle accidents, to being hit in the head with a liquor bottle.

It is a profession that comes with inherent risk, however we accept those risks and continue to serve our fellow man due to our sense of duty, pride, and honor.

If you ever wanted to look at all of the law enforcement related deaths in the country, visit web site www.odmp.com. This is the Officer Down Memorial Page, that lists every officer lost in the line of duty, coast to coast, as far back as into the 1800's. If possible, they have a photo attached to a short bio of the officer and the details that are known surrounding their death. If you check the site with any type of frequency, you will be amazed at the number of officers that are killed almost daily and you would never hear about it otherwise.

You can look at and get law enforcement death related stats for individual states and even break it down to single departments. The site also recognizes K-9's as officers and lists their deaths in the line of duty as well. I am very impressed with how well the site stays updated and the quickness in which they get an officer posted. It's a very humbling website to visit, when you see the number of actual officers killed almost every day.

When I was stationed at the State Police Academy, we had what was called the Officer Down Book for each class. As Staff Instructors, we would pick one student to be responsible for the upkeep and content of the book. Each morning, prior to the morning inspection, the student would log onto the Officer Down website and see if there were any new officer related deaths from any where in the country.

If there was a new officer down, the student would print out the bio and details surrounding the death and place the page in the book. Then, it was the student's responsibility to read the entire page to the class prior to the morning inspection. Some days there would be none to read, while other days there would be several.

A typical 16 week Basic Class, usually graduates approximately forty to forty five Officers, Deputies, and Natural Resource

Officers. During the last week of the program, we would take the students to the class room and make them stand behind their desks. Then an instructor would read the name from every fallen officer's bio in the book, starting with the beginning of the program. As a name was read, a student would then sit down. By the time the names are finished being heard there were usually only a few students left standing.

It was a great visual effect for the students to realize the risks associated with wearing a badge. It always surprised the students as to exactly how many officers had died in the line of duty just in their short sixteen week program.

In the year 2012, shortly after I had hung up my uniform, West Virginia lost two Troopers in the same incident. Not only did the loss crush my heart, it crushed the hearts of an entire state of Troopers.

One of the Troopers was a good friend with whom I had worked several crime scenes. He had over seventeen years as a Trooper and left behind a wife and several children. The other had been a student when I was stationed at the Academy, and often we would discuss baseball as he had pitched for a local college and I coached a high school team.

One evening the two were involved in a traffic stop on Interstate 79 in Clay County. As the two Troopers placed the driver in the back seat of their cruiser, a handgun was missed during their search of the driver. Both Troopers were shot, one died at the scene, the other a couple of days later. The shooter was able to escape the cruiser and later the same night, also shot a tow truck driver, and a deputy who was responding to the scene. The deputy had also been a student of mine at the Academy.

The impact of the incident was felt by so many people on so many levels across the whole state. It literally rocked the entire state to its very core. The sense of loss was felt by every Trooper who had ever worn the green uniform and a large majority of the citizens of our proud state.

One thing I was happy to see, the department made sure grief counseling was offered in the post incident. It was such a senseless act. A lot of the Troopers and other officers I talked to were having a really hard time digesting what had happened.

Here were two men dedicating their lives to protecting the citizens of the state. These were two men who walked with pride, honor, and integrity whether in uniform or not, every day. Either one of whom would have readily given the shirt off his 6back to any stranger who might need it.

The only thing they wanted was to make this a better world for us to live in.

They were two great men and outstanding Troopers.

They are gone, but never forgotten.

Rest Easy Brothers….

The Trooper's Final call
By C. R. Holbert

The uniforms are pressed, fresh off the rack,
Shiny badges all wrapped in a band of black.

A casket wrapped in The Flag of the Land,
Over which, Proudly, The Honor Guard does
stand.

A Fallen Trooper is in a state of rest,
As The Brotherhood come to pay their last
respects.

Heads are bowed as tears are shed,
A flowered wreath is laid at his head.

His life for another in order to save,
To the Brotherhood, the ultimate price, he
gave.

Comes time, for The Trooper's Call to Roll,
All respond, except for the last soul.

The radio crackles with an unanswered call,
Not once, but twice, silence is heard by all.

The Final Roll Call, he can not meet,
For now, his patrol is upon Heaven's streets.

The bag pipes play Amazing Grace,
As the casket's lid is locked into place.

In the name of Pride, Honor, and Sacrifice,
The Trooper had walked this path of life.

From evil, others he did tend,
As he did his duty till the very end.

Rest Easy My Brothers…

Fun Stuff

Even though law enforcement is filled with violence, death, and the never ending stress, it is without a doubt filled with funny moments. There is not a group that epitomizes the saying "Work hard, Play hard" more that a bunch of tight knitted officers who are absolutely not afraid to laugh at their Brother and Sister's expense. You will not find a profession that contains more pranksters and jokers than law enforcement.

I think this is just one more coping mechanism of the day to day stress of the job. What better way to make one of your co-workers laugh hysterically than to shoot a blast of pepper spray under the bathroom door as they try to do their business sitting on the toilet? I learned real quick to put a towel on the floor inside the door when I did my business.

There's also a rule that allows for the more something hurts, the funnier it is. It's especially true, if it's another person's pain and not your own. I'm not talking the kind of pain that leaves a person maimed or injured, just the kind of pain that is funny to laugh at. The pain may not always be a physical one, sometimes mental anguish can be even funnier.

There was a Trooper who liked to walk around and show his "Texas Belt Buckle". Basically he would pull just his scrotum out of his uniform pants and stand right beside you with it hanging out. He would giggle and laugh like a kid as he would say, "Hey guys, look at my belt buckle!"

It was funny at first, however after a few days, we all got tired of seeing his junk. At the end of our shift late one night, we were all standing around in the lot behind the detachment getting ready to go home. There was a Trooper from the Task Force with us who had not seen the "Belt Buckle" yet.

We all knew it was going to happen, and sure enough, "Hey man, you want to see my new belt buckle?"

"Sure, let's see it," was the reply.

So the offender turned his back to us as he prepared to once again air his goods for everyone to see. What he didn't see was the can of pepper spray in someone's hand.

He turned around, hands on his hips and smiled triumphantly, "Look!"

The smile lasted for about the duration of the two second blast of pepper spray he received to his groin. Then it was time for us to laugh as the tears came to his face and the screaming began.

The screaming lasted all the way inside the detachment, to the bathroom, and into the shower, uniform and all. The laughing lasted for weeks. As a matter of fact, years later, it's still funny. I'm laughing now.

Even though we all took great delight in his misery, we still loved the guy. We loved him so much, we would have readily given our own life for him without thinking twice about it. And even though we had filled his groin with so much pepper spray, it permanently stained his uniform pants orange, he loved us the same. He loved us to the point he would have given his life for our own without having to think twice about it.

That's how law enforcement is. Unconditional love for the Brother or Sister you stand shoulder to shoulder with and take on the evil of the world. No matter how much pain they inflict on you.

I mentioned there is also fun in causing mental anguish among your Brothers and Sisters. Sometimes, that's the best kind, to watch the confused look on their faces as they try to figure out is going on.

Every year in the state of West Virginia, every Trooper is required to go to the Academy for three days of In-Service training and recertification. Every Tuesday for several months brings a new group of approximately fifty Troopers to the Academy from all over the state.

The first day is always the longest as you are required to stay late for night fire on the range. And since the second day starts especially early for those who are getting physical exams, everybody is always in a hurry to get out of there.

One year, myself and another Trooper from the same detachment, were in the first relay to shoot, so we were getting ready to leave while quite a few were still up on the range. There were still at least forty blue and gold cruisers parked together on the Academy parking lot. They are all identical in looks with the only difference being the number on the license plate. Each Trooper is issued their own plate with their unit number on it and required to keep it on the rear of their car. In a large group of cruisers, usually the only way to find your car is by the number on the license plate.

As we were walking down the hill, I looked at my Buddy and said, "Look at all of these cruisers. Wouldn't it be funny if all of the license plates got switched around and nobody could find their own cruiser?"

And that is exactly what happened. We both grabbed screw drivers and randomly switched as many plates as we could before the next group finished shooting their relay. It was hilarious watching people walk to what they thought was their car and trying to figure out why the key would not unlock what they thought was their door.

Mental anguish, see, it's hilarious, the stuff never gets old.

There was a Trooper who was of a larger stature, and he often would remove his uniform shirt and put it on the back of his chair as he worked on his reports. As he was in the bathroom one morning doing his business, somehow his shirt got switched with one that was slightly smaller. His name tag, badge, and pins were put on the slightly smaller shirt and hung on the back of his chair. When he went to put his shirt on, he could barely get it buttoned up. He kept swearing and saying how he needed to go on a diet, he couldn't believe he had gained that much weight. When we went to have lunch, the rest of us ordered burgers and fries while he had a salad with no dressing. He walked around all day looking like the buttons were about to take flight off his chest. Finally at the end of the day, we gave his shirt back and had a good laugh.

Again, mental anguish, the fun never ends.

The best mental anguish for buddies to revel in, can often be the kind one inflicts on one's self.

When I was working in the southern part of the state, cell phone coverage was minimal at best. There were only a couple of spots in the whole county you could find one or two bars of service.

One afternoon, a Trooper got a speeder coming down a hill in a spot where of course there was no cell service. After going up to the offender's car to get his license, registration, and insurance, the Trooper went back to his cruiser only to find the doors were locked. No spare key, no cell service, keys in the car, and the doors locked.

Imagine the embarrassment of having to ask someone you were just about to write a ticket to, for a ride to the Department of Highways office several miles away so you can use their phone. And then, asking the same person to give you a ride back to your cruiser that is sitting on the side of the highway, engine running and blue strobes flashing with no one in it. Needless to say, the driver didn't get a ticket that afternoon.

One of my favorite's was when a Trooper left his cruiser unlocked and he ended up with a dead fish under his seat in the hot afternoon summer heat. The misery, and laughter, lasted for weeks as the smell refused to go away. I thanked the Good Lord above I had locked my cruiser doors and didn't get the fish.

That's how the Brotherhood is, you pick on each other mercilessly, but you have a devotion to each other that can not be described, only experienced. No words can express the true sense of support you have for each other during some of the most stressful times of your lives. That's why you need the laughter, to have a little release of the pressure.

Often the laughter came from the general public, for instance the time a drunken man walked into the Detachment and put several small pieces of soap on the counter. Then he stated he wanted to file a complaint of theft on the crack dealer who sold him the soap instead of $50 worth of crack. He demanded repeatedly for us to go get either his money or his crack. Needless to say the only thing he got was a ride to the jail for DUI as he had driven to the office to make his complaint. You can't make this stuff up!

We were having a vehicle safety check one evening when noticed a rolled joint behind a guy's ear. I instructed him to step out of the car and asked if he had any type of drugs in his possession. He emphatically replied no several times. Finally, I couldn't keep from laughing anymore as I reached up and pulled the marijuana joint from behind his ear, "Oh, you know I forgot all about that being there. Say, you're not going to tell my parole officer are you?"

"Uh, yes." Can you say "No more parole?"

When I was a deputy with the Lincoln County Sheriff's Office, I was trained as a K-9 Handler. One thing I learned very quickly is when you add a dog to the mix, the hilarity factor will go up quite a bit.

Blue was a one hundred twenty pound Chesapeake Bay Retriever, trained to locate drugs and as a tracking dog. He was a big dog with an even bigger personality, he loved the attention of working in the schools and more than anything, loved searching for drugs. He was awesome going through a building, full of energy while running his patterns and an absolutely excellent problem solver. He was very intelligent, to the point of being able to unlatch his kennel door until I put a lock on the latch.

Blue however, was not trained in bite work or apprehension. He was more likely to lick a criminal to death than bite one. But, if there was one thing bigger than his personality, it was his bark. It was a deep ferocious sounding bellow, and if you looked past his slobbery mouth, you would see his tail wagging the whole time he was sounding mean.

I had been training with him for several months before I was finally allowed to at least ride him around in the cruiser with me. I remember being very proud of him as I took him to the County Courthouse for the first time. As we walked into the office, the Sheriff yelled for me to come into his office.

"Boy, he sure is a great looking dog! Come here Blue!" exclaimed my boss.

And with that, the dog I was so proud of, hunkered his back and immediately dropped the biggest, pile of poop I had ever seem come out of an animal. It came out so quickly, I did not even have a chance to stop him. My mouth dropped to my knees as I stared at the big pile sitting on the carpet in front of the Sheriff's desk. I looked up and was speechless as Blue trotted over to the desk and placed his big paws up on the desk, with his tail wagging and started licking my boss. I cringed as I waited for the berating that was sure to follow. Then the Sheriff starting laughing and said, "I hope you know I'm not cleaning that up. Get to work!"

When I was finished, I came back into the office to find the Sheriff and Blue wrestling around. I was just glad Blue had made up for dropping a load in the middle of the office, even though it took some time for the smell to go away.

At that time I had a Durango as a cruiser with a cage behind the rear seat. Everything behind the back seat was Blue's area to ride. It was big enough for him to stretch his huge frame, yet tight enough to keep him restrained while running the rural roads of the county at high speeds.

One afternoon, Blue and I got called to a domestic in progress between a father and his adult son. The address was on a small single lane road pretty much in the middle of nowhere. It was a beautiful, early fall afternoon with a gentle breeze and a bright blue sky. I was enjoying the weather with all four windows rolled down, especially since Blue tended to fart a lot and I would rather smell the fall breeze than what he was blowing.

As I got close to the house, I saw the son take off on a bicycle, pedaling as hard as he could, trying to get away from me. He turned down an even smaller dirt side road as I hit the gas to catch up to him.

As I got close to him, he threw his bike down in the ditch and ran straight up the side of a mountain. And I mean it was pretty much straight up. I stopped the Durango and thought in amazement, "How in the world did he run up that steep hill that fast?"

Even though I was in great shape at the time, I couldn't help but think how bad it was going to suck trying to get up that steep incline. Then it happened, Blue cut loose with his loud bellowing. He was going nuts, to the point I turned and looked at him thinking something had to be wrong.

When I stopped the Durango I had been focused the guy running like a billy goat up the side of the hill. I didn't pay attention to the fact on the other side of my cruiser was a chicken coop. Blue was not paying a bit of attention to me or the man who had just beat up his own father. He was looking at those chickens and absolutely coming unglued for some reason.

Seeing my dog was alright, I quickly turned and started to run up the hill. Then I heard a terrified yell come down to me from way up above, "Please sir, don't put that dog on me! Please! I'm scared to death of dogs anyways! Please don't send him up here! I swear, I'm coming down with my hands up. I promise, I'm not fighting this time neither!"

"You had better get down here or else this big chewing machine is coming up to get you!" With that, I slapped the side of the cruiser knowing it would keep Blue barking.

Blue kept barking and never even looked at the guy, he was still wanting to play with the chickens.

I took the offender back to his house and finished my report with the family. The son, being in his forties, had become enraged at his parents when they had refused to give him money for pills. So his answer was to give his father a black eye and spit in his mother's face.

Then I put the handcuffed man in the back passenger side seat and buckled him in. He could see Blue's big slobbery head behind the cage, "Man, he's a big one. Are you sure he can't get to me in here?"

I reassured the fellow Blue would not get to him unless I gave the proper commands, never mind Blue had never bitten anything and was never trained to. But, when I put that guy in the back seat, there was just something about him that my big dog did not like. It was a thirty minute ride to the courthouse and the dog kept his mouth within inches of the back of that guy's neck and barked his ferocious slobbery bark the whole ride.

At one point I looked back to see this forty year old man in tears trying to lean forward in an effort to get away from the dog. He was literally crying like a baby. This man who had acted so tough to his own parents, had tears and snot running down his face.

Then about half way to the office, I smelled it. "Did you just crap your pants?"

"I'm so sorry Sir! I'm scared of dogs! I couldn't hold it! Please make him quit barking!"

I had never heard Blue bark so much, for some reason he did not like having this old country boy in the cruiser with us. That dog barked so much, by the time we got to the courthouse, he started sounding horse. As soon as we got to the courthouse and got Mr. Poopy out of the back seat, the barking stopped.

The best part was taking the tough guy to his arraignment wrapped in a garbage bag diaper. Afterwards, I took the Durango to the car wash to spray out my backseat. It was worth the dollar fifty it cost me in quarters to see the guy a little humiliated after having seen the way he treated his parents. What kind of a man would ever spit in his mother's face because she wouldn't give him money for pills?

The unpredictability of human nature is what could make things fun; you never knew what was going to happen from day to day.

I'm just glad I never had to look at another Texas Belt Buckle.

Goodness, I'm still laughing, it's the gift that keeps on giving.

Still love you Big Guy!

Routine Traffic Stop

Routine traffic stop.

There are no three words in law enforcement that could be further from the truth. I hate hearing those three words used together in any sense. Only people who have never actually initiated a traffic stop use those three words together.

There is nothing routine about the possibility of being injured or killed during a traffic stop. Very few things in law enforcement have more unknowns or have more potential to go sideways than putting those blue lights on behind a vehicle on the open road. A stop in broad daylight is just as dangerous as a stop in the middle of the night.

For a law enforcement officer, we have to have an entirely different mindset than what the average person realizes. When you get pulled over, you know who you are and what weapons are or are not in the car with you. That is what's completely unknown to the officer.

Yes, ninety percent of traffic stops are completed without any incident, however they are still not routine. That other ten percent outweighs the ninety by far when it comes to stress and danger. Because of that fact, every traffic stop has to be treated with the utmost caution and discretion.

From your position, you are probably worried about having to pay a speeding ticket, the officer has to worry about a hundred other things including if this a wanted murderer, is there a trunk full of guns, drugs, bombs, that is the unknown. That's why the officer is so cautious when approaching your vehicle.

It's not about automatically thinking you're a murderer, but there is always the chance you could be. Trust me, murderers drive cars just like you do. Officers don't have the luxury of knowing that information before hand.

I know one Trooper who was working the interstate on a nice sunny afternoon. It was one of those days in which a person can take great pleasure in just riding around with the windows down. The sky was blue, the temperature was nice and mild, with a gentle breeze blowing.

The Trooper was driving north and clocked a southbound driver a little over the speed limit. He turned around and initiated the traffic stop once catching up to the car. As the Trooper approached the car, he had no reason to suspect anything was wrong, until he got beside the rear window and looked inside to see a bound and gagged woman lying dead in the back seat.

The man had killed his wife earlier that day and was on his way to find a place to bury her body. The Trooper just happened to pull him over before he got to complete the job.

I have pulled cars over to only find out the driver was a wanted murderer from another state. Or the driver was drunk, or had a gun, or was wanted for parole violations. When you turn those blue lights on behind another vehicle, you never know what's going to happen.

I know, I know, you're sitting there thinking these are infrequent events and I'm exaggerating things. But, I'm really not.

Another Trooper I know pulled over a speeding car on the Turnpike one afternoon. Before the Trooper even made it out of his cruiser to approach the offender, the driver jumped out with a gun and started shooting at him. Looking at the post incident photos you can see several of the shots went through the headrest of the cruiser, right where his head would have been. Thank goodness the Trooper rolled out of his car and was able to return fire.

Every day all across the country these types of things are taking place. So, don't be offended when the officer acts so cautious while walking up to your car. Remember, all you have to worry about is paying a speeding fine, that officer has to worry about so much more, including his life.

One of the biggest things an officer needs to worry about is traffic. As people drive, they tend to steer in the direction they are looking. While the onlooker is stretching their neck to look at the pretty blue lights, they are also steering their car in that same direction. The next thing you know they plow into the vehicles parked on the side of the road often times injuring or killing somebody. I have had several friends hit by passing motorists during traffic stops.

As an accident reconstructionist, I often got called to complex accident scenes and fatalities to figure out exactly what happened and who was at fault. One night, I was called to the scene of a Trooper who was struck by a passing vehicle while working a traffic stop. It was a long drive for me and the Trooper had already been flown out by the time I got there.

The Trooper was training a new Academy graduate and they had pulled over a car on a small rural two lane road practically in the middle of nowhere. During the traffic stop, the driver was suspected to be intoxicated. The driver was brought back to the area between the two cars and asked to perform Field Sobriety tests. When the tests were completed the Trooper was going to retrieve the portable breathalyzer from inside the cruiser.

While watching the in car camera footage, you could see and hear everything transpiring during the stop. As he turned to go to the side of the car, the training officer looked at the new guy and said, "Make sure you are careful and not get hit by a passing car out here." Then he walks off screen to the driver's side of the cruiser, there is a thump and the car shakes a little. The next thing you see is a Trooper practically falls from the sky and lands at the feet of the new guy.

It was a hard thing to watch, I couldn't believe the time between the thump and seeing him land on the ground. He was in the air for a long couple of seconds before landing on the blacktop. My heart sank as I watched the event take place. The Trooper had been seriously injured and currently on his way to a trauma hospital in a helicopter. We were all praying he survived the accident.

The new guy was pretty shook up as it was his very first day on the job. He had just graduated from the Academy several days before. Now here he was trying to perform life saving first aid on his training officer who had just been struck by a car.

As I and another Trooper were wrapping up the scene, I walked up to take some good photos of the striking vehicle. You could see the indention in the front bumper where it had impacted the Trooper's legs. There was a dent in the hood where his body had slammed into it. Then I looked at the windshield, it was shattered and you could see the area where the Trooper had rolled across it and went airborne.

Then I noticed the green cloth from the uniform of a WV State Trooper was stuck in the glass of the car. There were little pieces of uniform wedged within the spider web of the shattered windshield.

Seeing those little pieces of cloth made my heart fall completely to my knees. This was one of my Brothers, the same uniform I proudly wore, and here I was looking at the little shredded pieces of his life.

I had to take a step back and clear my throat. I felt a resolve to make sure I worked the scene the best I could to make sure the driver that hit my Brother went to prison. Later that evening I learned the Trooper was going to survive, however he was going to have a long road to a full recovery.

Every officer working the road has had traffic stops that jumped sideways in the blink of an eye. It's part of the inevitable that's going to happen and what makes us so cautious on every stop.

Late one night in Logan County I was the working the road and decided to make a round through a small coal camp community outside the city of Logan. It was an area well known for drugs and violence as our calls for service were always frequent in the area.

As I turned to cross the small bridge into the little camp, a yellow Dodge van approached me from across a set of railroad tracks. The van was missing a headlight and started to make a left turn in front of me. I decided to stop the van for the equipment violation and flipped on my blue strobes and spotlights.

The van stopped directly in front of my cruiser at a forty five degree angle with the passenger side facing my car. I could see a female driver and male in the passenger seat. I called the stop in to the dispatch and got out to approach the van. Both occupants were sitting still with their hands in my line of sight, however something just didn't feel right as I got closer. I couldn't be sure, but they appeared to be talking under their breath to each other.

When I got to the back side of the passenger door and started to ask the passenger for his identification, suddenly the passenger side sliding door came open and another male jumped out grabbing my left arm. As I felt his grip tighten on me, the passenger door flew open and the other male jumped out grabbing my right arm. They instantly started pummeling with their fists as I began to fight back.

Then I heard the chilling words, "Get his gun!"

I fought to get my right hand on the butt of my pistol as I continued to hit back with my left fist. As soon as I felt the grip of my gun I hit the magazine release and dislodged the rounds of ammunition. On our weapons, once the magazine is unseated, the gun is rendered unable to fire. However I still was not going to let them have it.

I felt another set of hands on mine fighting for the weapon as I realized the female had exited the van and was now a part of the melee. All of this had taken approximately ten seconds to happen, but to me it felt like an eternity.

I remember getting furious at these three people as we struggled for possession of my gun. Who were they to try to take my gun? Who were they to disrespect me by hitting me? How dare they deny me the right to go home at the end of my shift? So many thoughts in a flurry as I continued to fight.

My Academy training took over as I yelled,"Back! Get Back!"

Muscle memory was kicking in as I started remembering the multiple assailant drills we went through at the Academy. I started concentrating on my breathing to make sure I didn't get hypoxic and pass out. I knew I was in better shape than these three, however the guy holding my right arm was definitely a lot stronger than the one on my left.

We were about fifteen seconds into the scuffle and it felt like two eternities at this point. I was able to get my foot up and shoved the female off of me, releasing her grip from my gun. I then pushed as hard as I could into the man on my right shoving him into the edge of the passenger front door of the van. I was able to get my arm free as he loosened his grip, then he took off running down the railroad tracks. I shoved the one on my left as hard as I could, causing him to release his grip on me and fall to the ground.

The female was now back on me grabbing at my uniform shirt. I shoved her off of me into the side of the van with such force, the side window exploded as it shattered.

Routine Traffic Stop my foot.

I never did catch the guy who ran down the railroad tracks, and neither of the other two were talking about who he was. But I at least got two of the three and was able to go home to my family at the end of the night.

In law enforcement that's what your goal is every day, to go home in one piece at the end of your shift. Outside of the military, you hardly have to worry about whether or not you are going to make it home at the end of your eight hours. Maybe you hate your job, boss, or co-workers, but do you really wonder if your family is going to see you in eight hours?

Every day I would get in my cruiser at the start of my shift and do two things, I said a prayer asking God for protection, then I pulled down my sun visor and looked at a picture of my family, and promised them I would be home as soon as I could at the end of my shift. Thankfully I never had to break that promise.

One of my Trooper Buddies at the Detachment gave me a hard time and razzed me about putting the female into the side window of the van. At least he did, until several weeks later when he got into a scuffle inside of a mobile home and put a guy into a large screen projector type television causing it to explode. Then it was my turn to laugh, funny how those things come around.

I averaged around one hundred traffic stops a month, so if ten percent of those have something happen, simple math says at least a couple stops a week will have an intoxicated driver, weapon, drugs, fugitive warrants, or any combination of variables that make it anything but "Routine."

One night I ran out of tickets and headed back to the Logan Detachment to get more. The ticket books are numbered and each Trooper is required to sign them out from the Detachment Commander's Office.

It had been a pretty busy evening and I had written quite a few tickets during my shift. It was approaching midnight so I decided to wrap up some paperwork real quick and head on to the house. I signed out a couple of fresh ticket books and got my paperwork submitted into the Sergeant's basket as I headed out the door.

I had about a thirty minute drive on a dark four lane road to get to my house at the time. I was just about to turn off the exit near home when the radar unit on my dash board started screaming a harsh tone indicating somebody was way above the sixty five mile an hour speed limit.

Suddenly a set of headlights came around the curve as I looked at the radar unit that was now showing an approaching speed of ninety miles an hour.

I went ahead and switched my blue strobes on as the car got close and waited for it to pass me so I could get behind. The car, a bright yellow Cavalier, immediately pulled over and shut its engine off.

The majority of the public is very respectful when pulled over. Most people realize the nicer they are, the less likely they are to get a ticket and will get to go home with a warning.

This guy was not a part of that majority. As I got to the driver's window, I was subjected to a berating before I even had an opportunity to say "Good evening." The man tore into me with a tongue lashing I had not heard since my days in the Academy. He informed how I needed to be catching real criminals and not bothering honest people on their way home from work. I heard how he paid my salary and hated it because his tax dollars could have been spent better hiring more garbage collectors. It went on and on as I stood there and let him vent. After a few minutes, he handed me his paperwork and told me to get back to my cruiser and "Do whatever it is you feel you need to do!"

I heard all of this without me even saying a word, as I took his verbal abuse and documentation back to my car. To be honest, I couldn't wait to get back to my cruiser, because this jerk was getting ready to get a stack of tickets. I was prepared for writer's cramps as I wrote statute after statute worth of citations for this loud mouth. I was going to write so many tickets to this fellow, his children would still be paying on them for him years later.

That is what I thought until I got in my cruiser and reached down for my ticket book. The very same ticket book I left on my desk at the Detachment, thirty minutes ago as I left to go home. My heart sank, if ever there was an individual who I wanted to write a bunch of tickets, it was this guy. I was out of tickets and it was so late, there was nobody around to bring me my books sitting on my desk.

What to do?

"Kindness! Hit him with kindness," something said in my head.

I took the man's license and paperwork back to his car. As I approached I could see him sitting there, as he heard me get closer, he held out his hand without looking and said, "Show me where to sign. I know you wrote me a ticket."

I smiled; put on the most passionate face I could, and spoke with a voice usually reserved for telling one of my children I was disappointed in their behavior. Then I stepped around to where the man could clearly see me and handed him his paperwork back.

"Sir, you have obviously had a rough day and I would really hate to compound whatever is bothering you. As a servant of the great State of West Virginia and its citizens, I feel it's my duty to give you a break tonight and not even write you a warning. I appreciate the feedback you gave me earlier and will consider it constructive criticism as I try to be a better Trooper in all of my future endeavors. I hope I have made your evening a little more bearable and reduced some of the stress you are obviously suffering from. Have a good night....Sir" The last sir came out through clinched teeth as I was trying to maintain my professional composure.

The man sat there and just stared at me like I had slapped him across the face, then he erupted in tears. Now it was my turn to be surprised.

"I just found out my mother died and was on my way from work to meet my family. I am so sorry for being mouthy, I wouldn't have blamed you for writing me a stack of tickets. Thank You Trooper."

I stood on the side of the road and watched the man drive off. I stood there by myself, as there was no traffic on the four lane road this time of night, and looked at my blue strobes reflecting from the hillside. Then I looked up, it was a perfectly clear night with a million stars in the sky. The night was absolutely silent, only the sound of my cruiser's engine idling could be heard.

I don't know why, but I wasn't meant to write that man a ticket, of that I feel sure. I had been so full of anger just a short time ago and now I felt nothing but compassion for the grief stricken fellow. If I would have written him a hundred tickets, I still would have gone home mad and aggravated. I was suddenly glad I had forgotten my ticket book. I was glad I had at least been a little positive moment in the middle of a terrible evening for an unknown stranger. Unknowingly, this stranger had also been a little positive time in my night.

I smiled as I walked back to my cruiser. I opened the door and paused for a second, chuckled, and said to no one, "Damn, it's sure great to be a West Virginia State Trooper."

You Can Stop Wearing The Uniform

But you can never stop being a Trooper....

It has now been almost five years since I hung up my uniform and I still go through every day with a Trooper's mentality. There are still times I feel like I have not fully decompressed. I am not sure I ever will. My time as a deputy and Trooper definitely had life long effects on me, some I am very proud of and others I would rather keep buried inside.

I am proud of the manner in which I walked my career and those I had a positive influence on while teaching at the Academy. I am very proud of the people I was able to help over the years, the stolen property I was able to get back, and the criminals I put in prison.

I feel I was destined in this life to serve others, to be a protector of those who may not be able to protect themselves. Between the US Navy and law enforcement, I have spent over twenty years wearing three different uniforms. Each was worn with the same sense of pride, honor, integrity, and dedication to others.

I have found old habits are definitely not easily forgotten. When I am at a restaurant or other public facility, I always sit where I can see the most people. And even though I am sitting and may look relaxed, my eyes never stop moving. I am looking and noticing every detail of those around me, watching every mannerism they exhibit.

While driving, I am constantly reading the registration plates of other vehicles. Every day I am seeing at least a dozen vehicles that I would want to pull over for one violation or another. Almost every day I am identifying an intoxicated driver, or a vehicle with expired tags.

While I was a Trooper, I drove a Ford Crown Vic as a cruiser; however I had not been inside one in the last four years. A couple of months ago I bought a nice, used Crown Vic ex-police cruiser. When I started using it as my daily driver, it was amazing the memories that were brought back the more I drove it. It's slate gray with a plain simple interior and black steel wheels. It is about as nondescript of a car as you could ever ask for.

But, it has a big motor, heavy suspension, yards of trunk space, and rides as smooth as silk. I love it.

It has certainly been a unique path I have walked over the years. I feel extremely blessed to have been able to see and experience a lot of the things I have in life. However, there are those things I can not but help wish I could forget. There were times laughing was the only I could keep from throwing up or shedding tears.

There have been a lot of things I closed away inside and only in the writing of this publication, brought back to the surface. You can't go through a career in law enforcement and not experience things and events you wish you could forget.

The atrocities that humans inflict on each other are unfathomable unless you have been there to see, experience, and even smell them. There is no way to explain the emotions and feelings involved in dealing with these same events.

At the time I experienced these events, I never really had time to fully deal with them. So, my way of coping was to lock everything behind a door inside. I have always envisioned it like a cartoon door with chains draped across it keeping everything locked away as the door bulges at the seams. Inside are all of the hurt, pain, tears, and things I never wanted to deal with.

While I was wearing my badge, I definitely experienced my share of the emotional roller coasters. However, it was not until after my career ended that I started to fully experience what I had been keeping locked away inside. It was as if the demons behind the locked door finally started to escape a little at a time.

I never experienced what I would call "Cop" dreams while I was still a Trooper, once I started to decompress a little, the dreams slowly started. Mainly they always revolve around me needing to use my service weapon, but it will never fire. Even though it is loaded and I am being shot at, I can never get my gun to work. Usually end up being shot by the individual I am trying to shoot.

Recently, since I began writing this manuscript, the dreams have gotten very graphic and increased in frequency and intensity. They are varied in content and emotion; very often having an ominously dark feeling to them. I always wake up feeling drained emotionally and often with severe headaches.

In the years after taking off my badge, I have fought depression, and severe feelings of loneliness. I also isolated myself from those around me because I did not want other people to see exactly what I was dealing with.

I was used to being viewed as a big tough guy who would take on the evil of the world. I suddenly found myself embarrassed by the fact my emotions were kicking my butt.

It has taken several years for me to deal with these feelings on my own. It was only when I felt like I was getting somewhat back to normal, did I start to get the desire to put these words out to the public. I have always heard writing is therapeutic, to be honest, I'm not sure if it is. In putting my thoughts on paper, I have opened old wounds and feelings to only relive them again.

In looking back, I can honestly say I wish I would have found somebody to talk to. Somebody who could have helped me process what I was going through personally and emotionally.

My advice to others would be give yourself as much time as possible to process the things you experience. Take your time off for your family and spend as much time as possible with them. When I left the department, I had accumulated over twelve weeks of unused vacation time. Time, I should have taken to spend with my kids. Instead I gave up time off because I felt my sense of duty would not allow me to leave for a week at a time. I was wrong.

I think those weeks off would have given me a little time away from the day to day stresses to deal with and process things. I think this is also one reason it has taken me so long to start feeling decompressed since leaving law enforcement behind.

I am very proud to have helped so many people during my time toeing the line; I just wish I would have taken a little more time to help myself along the way.

Post Script

Earning my green uniform was without a doubt the proudest thing I have ever accomplished other than being a father. I have been extremely privileged to have had some of the best Troopers in the country by my shoulders in some of the darkest situations a person could ever have imagined.

Law enforcement is so much more than just a job, a paycheck, or a career. It's family. It truly is a gathering of Brothers and Sisters. I used to preach "We are all that we have" to my students at the Academy. In the world of being an officer, deputy, or trooper, it's true.

It's rare for law enforcement to have real friends outside the realm of the badge. This is certainly not meant as an offense against anybody without a badge. It's just cops understand cops, and rarely trust anybody who does not wear a uniform.

You see, we don't necessarily walk the same path of life as everybody else. When you pin a badge to your chest and strap a gun around your waist every day, you have to have a different mind set. Places where most people see a safe environment, we see the opportunity for madness and mayhem.

I had somebody complain about me to the Pastor at the church I used to attend. Evidently another member had seen the butt of my weapon inside my suit jacket and felt the House of the Lord was the not the place for a firearm. He complained to the Pastor, who in turn, talked to me about it. I was nice when approached about the issue, because I understand not everybody has the same mentality as I do. I never did tell the Pastor I would stop wearing the weapon, from that point forward, I just wore my compact .45 on my ankle. There were no more complaints, as I just did a better job of hiding my gun.

I hope in reading this, You, the Reader, now have a little better understanding of what makes officers click, the motivations, the stress, and the after math endured by not only the officer, but the family as well. Hopefully you have a little different mind set the next time you get pulled over for a traffic stop and the officer is being very cautious at your car window.

Maybe the officer is not as pleasant in speaking to you as you feel he should be. You never know, he may have just had to pick up a dead infant from a crib and put it in a body bag. His mind may not only be on the traffic stop you are mutually involved in, but also the small child at home waiting patiently to pass baseball when he gets there. The child he desperately wants to get home to so he can hug him and say how thankful he is to have the child safe and sound.

You may know you do not have any ill intent, but the officer has to assume you do. If he doesn't, then the next person he deals with may kill him.

And most of all, please do not forget the families standing beside the officer, supporting him or her. Without the family sacrificing their time with their loved one, we as Americans would not enjoy the sense of security and protection we have across this great land.

What you have read in this publication is really just the tip of the iceberg in the things I experienced during my time in law enforcement. Even though some of the things you just read may seem extraordinary, they are really the ordinary. My story, feelings, stresses, and emotions, are shared by many. Every day the men and women of law enforcement in this country are being subjected to ever increasing stress and danger. Every day the proud Brothers and Sisters trying to make a difference are not getting the support they need and deserve.

I have walked my portion of the line and now it's time to allow the next generation of officers to have their time on the path of blue. To them, I say hold your head high and be proud of the heritage left by those who have already cleared the path before you. Be proud, keep your honor, and maintain your integrity.

My shift has come to an end.

I'm 10-7, 10-42, Out of Service and Off Duty.

The following is an excerpt from the first book in my new fiction Series, "The Trooper".

Nate Johnson is a retired State Trooper fighting bad guys and the demons that come with over twenty years of wading through the violence, blood, and guts of the backwoods of West Virginia. After losing his best friend to an ambush, and now working as a private investigator, Nate takes on the rough cases no one else will touch. Working with vengeful like determination, Nate is often left wondering,
"Which side of the law am I walking now?"

The Trooper

It was a beautifully clear fall night....nice and cool, not a cloud in the sky, with a big full moon. Nate Johnson took in a full breath of the sweet air, you could taste the upcoming winter. Staring up, he watched as the flashing light of a commercial jet traveled across the sky. Then he looked down at It....

It looked fast just sitting there....sparkling red paint and shiny, chrome side pipes. You could see the recently installed, oversized disc brakes through the spokes of the polished aluminum racing wheels.

And it was fast, very fast, the beefed up engine was thumping over four hundred fifty horsepower before the one hundred shot of nitrous kicked in. All of this power flowed through an after market five speed transmission to the reinforced rear end and down to the pavement on the sticky Goodyear tires.

God, he loved this car....

He had grown up with the dream of some day owning a Third Generation Corvette, and here it was. He purchased the 1976 Corvette from an elderly man who had owned it since new. It had taken eight thousand dollars to purchase his dream and had been worth every penny. Nate had spent another almost ten thousand dollars upgrading everything from the suspension to the brakes. Again, it had been worth every penny. It completely emptied his savings account and even taken a few savings bonds to get the car the way he wanted.

It was just past midnight of another sleepless night. There had been plenty of those lately, ever since the shooting. Ever since he had to face the killers of his best friend and traded gun fire face to face with them. Ever since he had to pull into that familiar drive way and deliver the message to his best friend's wife. The message nobody wanted to deliver, much less hear.

He refused his own trip to the emergency room until he had delivered the message himself. Brett had been his best friend and this task was his responsibility and his alone. The Major had thrown a fit at the scene because he would not get in the ambulance and take the ride to the hospital. However, he was pretty sure the Major had understood when he had been politely told to go screw him self, nobody else was delivering this message.

He looked again at the car, the windows were down and the t-tops off. The red leather interior was still like new and he could smell the leather conditioner he used earlier in the day after washing and waxing his dream car. The smell of the wax was still on his hands from the three hours spent polishing every square inch of paint and chrome.

Several minutes ago, Nate had stepped into the night air to pull the car back into the garage. Now he just stood staring at it sitting next to the blue and gold colored Ford Crown Vic Cruiser with the markings of a West Virginia State Trooper. It was dark and silent as it sat there looking even more menacing than the Vette. The whip antennae pointed silently into the night sky waving back and forth gently in the gentle breeze. The cruiser had not been moved in over a week, not since that night, that life changing night.

He stepped down from the porch toward the driveway and immediately winced and buckled slightly as the sharp pain of his right knee gripped him. The doctor had told him he would carry some of the buckshot for the rest of his life. The surgeons had spent several hours picking the lead pellets from his right leg. Lucky for him the shooter had loaded the shotgun with birdshot and not something heavier. Still the several hundred pellets had left his right pant leg shredded and him bleeding heavily from all of the holes as the hot lead had pierced his skin.

He walked across the sidewalk to the Vette sitting in the driveway and ran his hand across the hood. He loved the feel of the smoothness left behind by the wax. It felt almost like a woman's skin, silky smooth and vibrant to his touch. He closed his eyes as he kept his hand on the hood. It almost felt alive, there was a pulse softly beating under his hand, as he felt the vibrancy of the horsepower lying just beneath the hood. It beckoned him, whispered his name softly, and begged to be unleashed. It was time for a ride.

He opened his eyes and walked behind the Vette to the driver's side door next to the Blue and Gold. He pushed down on the door handle and looked over at the cruiser to the dried red clay mud slung along the bottom of the rocker panels. That wet, muddy unnamed road he had driven so hard across to answer the yells of "Signal Five, Signal Five, Officer needs assistance! Shots Fired! I am taking shots from three individuals."

He opened the door to the Corvette and slid into the smooth red leather seat behind the steering wheel. He looked again at the mud as he shut the door and thought once more of the bumpy ride across the old logging road. He had pushed the cruiser as hard as it had ever been driven, in a desperate attempt to get to the scene. He remembered screaming into the microphone that he was on his way, to hold on, the Calvary was coming and bringing Hell with it.

The key slid silently into the ignition and the softly glowing dash lights illuminated as he turned the key to the first click. He paused for a brief moment, then pushed the key, feeling the Vette vibrate as the side pipes roared to life. He looked at the gauges ensuring everything was operating as it should be. The headlights popped up like the eyes of a frog as he pulled out the switch. He gave the accelerator a tap and watched as the gauges jumped. God, he loved this car.

The Vette vibrated slightly as the high friction racing clutch took hold and slowly pushed the sleek red car backwards into the street. With a slight tap of the gas and a quick change of the gears, The Beast rumbled even more as it moved forward down the street toward the main drag.

He let the car idle down the street in first gear, the pipes gurgling as the spent high octane fuel fumed out the open tips. Another quick check of the gauges proved everything was as it should be as the Vette growled past the stop sign. Turning left onto Main Street, the RPM's came up smoothly through the progression of the gear changes as the speedometer started to climb. The soft night air billowed through the open tops bringing with it smells of the approaching fall time.

Keeping the speed at thirty five also kept the car in third gear as the red rocket crept through the sleeping town. He looked over at the empty passenger seat and thought of his best friend. A smile spread across his face as he remembered the last time Brett had been sitting there. The side pipes had just been installed and he wanted to show them to his best friend on the way home. The Vette sounded like a roaring lion as he had pulled into the driveway revving the engine to the point the windows of Brett's house were vibrating. The commotion had brought the whole family outside to see what monstrous machine had been brought to their calm household.

Brett had demanded a ride right then and there much to the dismay of his wife. Brett's ten year old son, nicknamed Little Terry, stood in the front yard demanding a burnout as the two were pulling away. Laughing he remembered how Brett had grabbed the dashboard after he dropped the accelerator, boiling the rubber from the Goodyear tires through the first three gears. Little Terry had been jumping up and down squealing as his mommy tried to get him inside the house, and away from the heavy smoke left behind in the air.

The approaching red light brought him back to the present as he tapped the brakes and down shifted. As the shifter slid into second gear, the light turned green, green like the uniform of a Trooper, reminding him of the first time the two had earned the right to wear The Green of West Virginia.

He and Brett had started on the same day at the Sheriff's department and quickly became best friends as the two went through The Academy together. After several years, it had been Brett who convinced him to go back for another thirty weeks to earn the right to wear the uniform of a West Virginia State Trooper. The training had been extremely tough and the two had come to rely on each other heavily throughout, solidifying their Brotherly love for each other even more.

The Vette jumped forward as it was pushed through the gears, accelerating quickly to the posted speed limit of fifty five miles per hour. The night air billowed even more through the cockpit as the speed increased. The air washed across his face as he steadied the accelerator to halt the speedometer's climb. The Beast was begging to be unleashed; he could feel the horsepower thunder as the engine beat out its loud tune through the pipes.

"I'm hit! There are three of them! They ambushed me! How far out are you?" came a yell over the cruiser's radio speaker.

"I'm almost there! Hold on, I'm coming as fast as I can!" He yelled into the microphone completely forgetting all radio protocol, "Where are they in relation to your position? I can see your blue lights up ahead! Hold on Buddy!"

Then came the chilled reply, "Jesus....One is right here in front of me."

Tears swelled in his eyes as he noticed the sign ahead advertising the approach of the Interstate 64 on-ramp. A down shift and slight jerk of the steering wheel put him heading west towards Huntington as he progressed back up through the gears. A reflection of a star shaped decal brought his attention back in focus as he backed off the accelerator half way up the ramp. Then he saw the words, Sheriff's Department, across a trunk deck lid, there was a Deputy sitting on the shoulder in the dark with his lights out.

He knew the game as he had played it to perfection many times his self. The object was to sit in the dark and wait to nail somebody for speeding. The cruiser was facing forward and looking through the back glass could be seen the red numbers of the RADAR unit sitting on the dash.

Dropping another gear brought the Vette's speed even lower as The Red Beast approached the cruiser parked on the right hand shoulder at the end of the ramp.

"Screw it!" Nate thought as the Corvette came even with the parked Deputy.

Suddenly, he jammed the accelerator to the floor as he pulled back into second gear. The open side pipes yelled a thunderous roar as every bit of horse power was suddenly unleashed and the sticky Goodyear tires screamed in fury trying to find traction that did not exist. A quick speed shift into third gear brought the speed up as the tachometer needle pushed into the red zone.

He screamed as the on rush of emotions ripped through his chest and out his mouth. "I was supposed to be there to take the bullet for him!"

By the time the Corvette hit the interstate, the speedometer was showing over one hundred miles an hour and rapidly climbing.

Blue lights flashed in his rear view mirrors, as the Deputy got over crapping his pants and jumped into action. Nate was sure there was a stress filled voice calling a pursuit in to the Putnam County dispatcher at that very moment.

Blue lights…. "Jesus….One's right here in front of me."

Nate's cruiser's lights picked up the scene as it played out if front of him. There was an old red pick up sitting cross ways completely blocking the old unnamed logging road. Evidently it had been parked in a manner to attempt an ambush of Brett as he had chased the truck into the back woods.

Evidently when Brett had slid to a stop, he never knew the fleeing driver and passengers had jumped out of the truck and were standing in the brush beside the driver side of the cruiser. As Brett was scampering out of his car, the suspects had blindsided him with blasts from their guns, almost knocking him back into his cruiser. Thus began a short exchange of gun fire between the three and Brett, with the Trooper shooting almost blindly into the dark brush at the suspects.

The blue lights grew dimmer in his rear view mirrors as the speedometer jumped past one hundred twenty miles per hour. The Vette lurched even faster forward as Nate brought the gear shift back up into fifth gear and pushed the accelerator pedal harder to the floor. Tears were streaming down his cheeks now. God….Why?

Blue lights…. "Jesus….One's right here in front of me."

Brett was sitting on the ground leaning back within the open door jam of his cruiser, one of the gunmen was standing over top of him about five feet away pointing a shotgun at his chest. The blue flashing lights of Brett's cruiser filled the air, as Nate slid to a stop. He grabbed his AR-15 jumping out of the cruiser as the suspect's shotgun roared, tearing into Brett's body. Immediately, gunfire erupted from Nate's left side as the remaining gunmen had been laying in wait in the dark brush with what sounded like another shotgun and a handgun.

Something hit Nate in his upper chest like the kick of a mule, instantly he realized his body armor had probably just saved his life by stopping a bullet.

Blue lights on the interstate up ahead indicated the presence of several additional cruisers. Nate realized the Deputy behind him must have radioed ahead for assistance. He was quickly approaching the Winfield exit, as the flashing blue lights up ahead showed they were trying to quickly set up a road block under the overpass. Undoubtedly, they would have the stop strips out to deflate his tires. The problem for them, was the road block was fifty yards past the exit ramp.

Brett was flung backward by the force of the shotgun blast, then, the gun roared a second time and Brett lay still.

He downshifted and pulled the wheel slightly to the right, shooting the Vette up the exit ramp avoiding the roadblock. Again the emotions roared out of his mouth as the engine roared into the red zone.

"No!" He screamed as another roar of gunfire tore through the night, this time in his direction.

He was fast approaching the top of the ramp as another set of flashing blue lights could now be seen fast approaching from the right. The tears were flowing steady now, emotions rolling down his cheeks. The blue lights turned away from him going down the on ramp obviously without the knowledge he had taken the exit ramp.

He could hear the shotgun pellets scattering around him. He was bringing the AR-15 up level as the shotgun in the brush roared again and he felt the heavy thump of the pellets striking his legs with the right one taking the brunt of the load. He slightly staggered as he started to send screaming .223 rounds back in the direction of another flash from the shotgun barrel to his left. The shotgun had to be out of ammo, he thought hopefully as he sent another volley of AR-15 rounds at the suspects. Suddenly, the one that *had been standing over Brett turned and ran into the darkness of the woods.*

Then all shooting stopped and was replaced by silence.

The Vette fish tailed through the intersection as he jerked the steering wheel to the left. He could see the deputies down below were realizing their mistake and trying hard to get their cruisers back up the on ramp. With a down shift and another jerk of the wheel to left, the Vette screamed as it shot down the east bound on ramp like a run a way freight train. As the speed again crossed the one hundred mile an hour mark, the cool fall air blew the full tears back across his cheeks.

Quiet....just the flashing blue lights....as Nate squatted down on one knee, he realized it was quiet. The smell of gunpowder was in the air as he cautiously approached the rear of Brett's cruiser.

The flashing blue lights were on the other side of the interstate going up the on ramp as he was hitting fifth gear, crossing one hundred twenty miles an hour on the speedometer going in the opposite direction.

Nate crept past Brett's cruiser and cleared the red truck of passengers or any other shooters. Returning back to Brett, while being mindful of the gunmen returning, he looked at his fallen best friend and wept.

Surely they would try another road block ahead if they were able to get the cars set up in time. He needed to get to the next exit before them he thought as he mashed the accelerator even harder. He could hardly see as the tears flowed freely now.

The driveway was empty as Nate pulled up to the house and shut off the engine. It had taken the medics about an hour to get him patched up enough to be able to make the drive to Brett's house. There was a light on where he knew was the living room. He thought briefly of how proud Brett had been to buy the modest home. A face appeared in the blinds of the living room, it was Brett's wife Linda. Brett always said she waited up for him no matter how late he came home because she worried often about him.

There were no blue lights as he quickly approached the next exit ramp. Another quick flick of the steering wheel and he was shooting up the ramp, still no blue lights.

He opened the cruiser door and exited, almost tripping over Little Terry's bicycle lying on its side. He remembered helping Brett put it together for Christmas. The boy had been delighted when he saw it next to the tree on Christmas morning. He set the small bike up and pushed it away from the driveway. Nate pulled on his campaign hat low over his eyes as the front door of the house opened, "Brett, get in here and give your wife a kiss!" Then, the look of realization, "Where's Brett?"

The flashing blue lights could be seen dimly in the back ground of the dark rear view mirrors. Only a few more miles to the house and the safety of the garage. Suddenly, there were flashing blues every where as he came around a bend in the road.

Nate stopped instantly in his tracks, he didn't have to say a word. She knew immediately. "He's not coming home, is he?" The screams of anguish had been loud enough to bring Little Terry downstairs out of his bed. Then it got real bad. God....Why?

Then the thought came again....Screw it. The tears were flowing and his voice was screaming as he down shifted and pushed the accelerator to the floor. The roar of the exhaust pipes drowned everything else out.

He had stayed at the house until Linda's parents got there to help and Little Terry was back in bed. Only then did he take the ride to the hospital to endure several hours of effort to remove as many of the tiny pellets as possible from his right leg.

Suddenly he saw there was a gap between the cruisers! He could see a Deputy coming around the back of one of the cars carrying a set of stop sticks. They had not had time to get the stop strips out! The Deputy barely had time to jump back as the red Vette screamed through the gap.

Troopers from across the country came to the funeral. It was a beautiful fall day with two enormous American flags hanging from the buckets of two fire trucks. Birds chirped as the bag pipes played Amazing Grace, while the honor guard placed Brett in the horse drawn hearse to take him to the cemetery.

Even with a knee full of lead pellets and over two hundred fresh stitches, Nate stood as part of the Honor Guard. No amount of pain or stitches was going to keep him from being next to Brett one last time.

He pulled the Vette into the garage, shut the engine off, and got out of the driver's seat. Walking out to the driveway while wiping the tears from his face, he could see the Deputy's cruisers scream past the intersection and continue down Main Street.

Nate had been able to hold himself together pretty well emotionally until he and the Honor Guard folded the American Flag which had draped Brett's coffin. Once the flag was folded into a tight triangle, Nate turned sharply, and saluted Brett's family. Tears could now be seen streaming down the big Trooper's face from underneath his sunglasses. He lowered his salute and then knelt to present the flag to Linda. As Nate held the flag forward, suddenly Little Terry stood and saluted his father's coffin.

Tears came to everyone's eyes.

Made in the USA
Columbia, SC
10 March 2022

57492858R00105